ON THE JOB SERIES

REAL PEOPLE WORKING in

SCIENCE

Jan Goldberg

D1507562

VGM Career Horizons

NTC/Contemporary Publishing Group

Library of Congress Cataloging-in-Publication Data

Goldberg, Jan.
    Real people working in science / Jan Goldberg.
       p.   cm.—(On the job series)
    ISBN 0-8442-4719-7 (hc).—ISBN 0-8442-4720-0 (pbk.)
    1. Science—Vocational guidance.   2. Engineering—Vocational
guidance.   3. Scientists—Interviews.   4. Engineers—Interviews.
I. Title. II. Series.
Q147.G65   1998
502'.3—dc21
                                        97-41634
                                             CIP

This book is dedicated to the memory of my parents,
Sam and Sylvia Lefkovitz.

Published by VGM Career Horizons
A division of NTC/Contemporary Publishing Group, Inc.
4255 West Touhy Avenue, Lincolnwood (Chicago), Illinois 60646-1975 U.S.A.
Copyright © 1998 by NTC/Contemporary Publishing Group, Inc.
All rights reserved. No part of this book may be reproduced, stored in a retrieval
system, or transmitted in any form or by any means, electronic, mechanical,
photocopying, recording, or otherwise, without the prior permission of
NTC/Contemporary Publishing Group, Inc.
Printed in the United States of America.
International Standard Book Number: 0-8442-4719-7 (cloth)
                                      0-8442-4720-0 (paper)
15   14   13   12   11   10   9   8   7   6   5   4   3   2   1

Contents

Acknowledgments

The author gratefully acknowledges the following:

- The numerous professionals who graciously agreed to be profiled in this book

- My dear husband Larry for his inspiration and vision

- My children, Deborah, Bruce, and Sherri, for their encouragement and love

- Family and close friends—Adrienne, Marty, Mindi, Cary, Michele, Paul, Michele, Alison, Steve, Marci, Steven, Brian, Jesse, Bertha, Aunt Estelle, Uncle Bernard, and Aunt Helen for their faith and support

- Diana Catlin, for her insights and input

- Betsy Lancefield, editor at VGM, for making all projects rewarding and enjoyable

How to Use This Book

On the Job: Real People Working in Science is part of a series of career books designed to help you find essential information quickly and easily. Unlike other career resources on the market, books in the *On the Job* series provide you with information on hundreds of careers, in an easy-to-use format. This includes information on:

- The nature of the work
- Working conditions
- Employment
- Training, other qualifications, and advancement
- Job outlooks
- Earnings
- Related occupations
- Sources of additional information

But that's not all. You'll also benefit from a firsthand look at what the jobs are really like, as told in the words of the employees themselves. Throughout the book, one-on-one interviews with dozens of practicing professionals enrich the text and enhance your understanding of life on the job.

These interviews tell what each job entails, what the duties are, what the lifestyle is like, what the upsides and downsides are. All of the professionals reveal what drew them to the field and how they got started. And, to help you make the best career choice for yourself, each professional offers you some expert advice based on years of experience.

Each chapter also lets you see at a glance, with easy-to-reference symbols, the level of education required and salary range for the featured occupations.

So, how do you use this book? Easy. You don't need to run to the library and bury yourself in cumbersome documents from the Bureau of Labor Statistics, nor do you need to rush out and buy a lot of bulky books you'll never plow through. All you have to do is glance through our extensive table of contents, find the fields that interest you, and read what the experts have to say.

Introduction to the Field

"Curiosity killed the cat"—or so the saying goes. But curiosity has been responsible, at least in part, for countless inventions, vaccines for a number of diseases, and a host of devices considered a normal part of our modern technology. It is curiosity that is at the very heart of a scientist's world.

Always at work searching for new information, scientists use their creativity, curiosity, and knowledge to proceed in their search for answers to questions. Like detectives, they read, collect, and process data as they seek out clues that will help solve the many mysteries of life. Using patience and determination, they repeat experiments again and again. Why is grass green? Where do rocks come from? Why does a volcano erupt? What causes diabetes? Why are some people allergic to bee stings? How small can an operating computer be?

Scientists must be patient and prepared for failure because often years are required prior to success (and sometimes that success is never realized). Scientists build upon both the successes and failures of others in their field. For example, before Jonas Salk developed his polio vaccine, many scientists worked long and hard to understand what caused this disease and how it could be prevented.

All of the careers outlined in this book have some things in common, but they are nevertheless distinctly different. Read through the chapters to hone in on the differences, and pay special attention to the interviews of individuals who are working in the field. They will provide you with special insights about the day-to-day life of performing that job. As you are perusing the book, ask yourself the following questions:

- How much time and money am I willing to devote to prepare myself for this career?

- Do I enjoy working with people, or am I happier working on my own?

- Am I a curious person?

- Do I enjoy problem solving?

- Do I want a nine-to-five job, or am I willing to work longer hours?

- Do I enjoy working outdoors—at least part of the time?

- Am I persistent—even in the face of failures?

- How well do I work under stress?

- Am I able to deal well with deadlines?

- Do I have strong communications skills?

- Am I willing to relocate in order to advance my career?

- Am I a patient and resilient professional?

This book will provide valuable information on working conditions and lifestyles so that you can make good choices based upon reliable facts.

Although *On the Job: Real People Working in Science* strives to be as comprehensive as possible, not all jobs in this enormous field have been covered or given the same amount of emphasis. If you still have questions after reading this book, there are a number of other avenues to pursue. You can find more information by contacting the sources listed at the end of each chapter or by locating professionals to talk to and observe as they go about their work. Any remaining gaps in your understanding of a particular occupation can be filled by referring to the *Occupational Outlook Handbook.*

CHAPTER 1 Careers in the Life Sciences

OVERVIEW
Biological and Medical Scientists

Biological and medical scientists are involved in the study of living organisms and their relationship to their environment. Most of these professionals specialize in some area of biology such as zoology (the study of animals) or microbiology (the study of microscopic organisms).

Many biological scientists and virtually all medical scientists work in the area of research and development. Some conduct basic research to increase our knowledge of living organisms. Others, in applied research, use knowledge provided by basic research to develop new medicines, increase crop yields, and improve the environment. Biological and medical scientists who conduct research usually work in laboratories using electron microscopes, computers, thermal cyclers, and a wide variety of other equipment. Some professionals may conduct experiments on laboratory animals or greenhouse plants. A number of biological scientists perform a substantial amount of research outside of laboratories. For example, a botanist may do research in tropical rain forests to see what plants grow there, or an ecologist may study how a forest area recovers after a fire.

Some biological and medical scientists work in management or administration. They may plan and administer programs for testing foods and drugs, for example, or direct activities at zoos or botanical gardens. Some biological scientists work as consultants to business firms or to government, while others write for technical publications or test and inspect foods, drugs, and other products. Some work in sales and service jobs for companies that manufacture chemicals or other technical products.

Advances in basic biological knowledge, especially at the genetic and molecular levels, continue to spur the field of biotechnology forward. Using this technology, biological and medical scientists manipulate the genetic material of animals or plants, attempting to make organisms more productive or disease resistant. The first application of this technology occurred in the medical and pharmaceutical areas. Many substances not previously available in large quantities are now beginning to be produced by biotechnological means; some may be useful in treating cancer and other diseases. Advances in biotechnology have opened up research opportunities in almost all areas of biology, including commercial applications in agriculture and the food and chemical industries.

Most biological scientists who come under the broad category of biologist are further classified by the type of organism they study or by the specific activity they perform, although recent advances in the understanding of basic life processes at the molecular and cellular levels have blurred some traditional classifications.

AQUATIC BIOLOGISTS Aquatic biologists study plants and animals that live in water. Marine biologists study saltwater organisms and limnologists study freshwater organisms. Marine biologists are sometimes erroneously called oceanographers, but oceanography usually refers to the study of the physical characteristics of oceans and the ocean floor.

BIOCHEMISTS Biochemists study the chemical composition of living things. They try to understand the complex chemical combinations and reactions involved in metabolism, reproduction, growth, and heredity. Much of the work in biotechnology is done by biochemists and molecular biologists because this technology involves understanding the complex chemistry of life.

BOTANISTS Botanists study plants and their environment. Some study all aspects of plant life; others specialize in areas such as identification and classification of plants, the structure and function of plant parts, the biochemistry of plant processes, the causes and cures of plant diseases, and the geological ancestry of plants.

MICROBIOLOGISTS Microbiologists investigate the growth and characteristics of microscopic organisms such as bacteria, algae, or fungi. Medical microbiologists study the relationship between organisms and disease or the effect of antibiotics on microorganisms. Other microbiologists may specialize in virology (the study of viruses), immunology (the study of mechanisms that fight infections), or environmental, agricultural, or industrial microbiology. Many microbiologists use biotechnology as they advance knowledge of cell reproduction and human disease.

PHYSIOLOGISTS Physiologists study life functions of plants and animals, both in the whole organism and at the cellular or molecular level, under normal and abnormal conditions. Physiologists may specialize in functions such as growth, reproduction, photosynthesis, respiration, or movement, or in the physiology of a certain area or system of the organism.

ZOOLOGISTS Zoologists study animals—their origin, behavior, diseases, and life processes. Some zoologists experiment with live animals in controlled or natural surroundings, while others dissect dead animals to study their structure. Zoologists are usually identified by the animal group they study, such as ornithology (birds), mammalogy (mammals), herpetology (reptiles), and ichthyology (fish).

ECOLOGISTS Ecologists study relationships among organisms and between organisms and their environments, including the effects of influences such as population size, pollutants, rainfall, temperature, and altitude.

MEDICAL SCIENTISTS Biological scientists who do biomedical research are usually called medical scientists. Medical scientists working on basic research delve into the functioning of normal biological systems in order to understand the causes of, and discover treatment for, diseases and other health problems. Medical scientists often try to identify the kinds of changes in a cell, chromosome, or gene that signal the development of medical problems, such as different types of cancer. After identifying structures of or changes in organisms that provide clues to health problems, medical scientists may then work on the treatment of problems. For example, a medical scientist involved in cancer research might try to formulate a combination of drugs that will lessen the effects of the disease. Medical scientists who have a medical degree might then administer the drugs to patients in clinical trials, monitor their reactions, and observe the results. (Medical scientists who do not have a medical degree normally collaborate with a medical doctor who deals directly with patients.) The medical scientist might then return to the laboratory to examine the results and, if necessary, adjust the dosage levels to reduce negative effects or try to induce even better results. In addition to using basic research to develop treatments for health problems, medical scientists attempt to discover ways to prevent health problems. Preventative medical research has, for example, affirmed the links between smoking and lung cancer and between alcoholism and liver disease.

TRAINING

For biological scientists, a Ph.D. degree generally is required for college teaching, independent research, and advancement to administrative positions. A master's degree is sufficient for some jobs in applied research and for jobs in management, inspection, sales, and service. A bachelor's degree is adequate for some nonresearch jobs. Some graduates with a bachelor's degree start as biological scientists in testing and inspection or get jobs related to biological science such as technical sales or service representative positions. In some cases, graduates with a bachelor's degree are able to work in a laboratory environment on their own projects, but this is unusual. Some may work as research assistants. Others become biological technicians, medical laboratory technologists, or, with courses in education, high school biology teachers. Many with a bachelor's degree in biology enter medical, dental, veterinary, or other health profession schools. Some enter a wide range of occupations with little or no connection to biology.

Most colleges and universities offer bachelor's degrees in biological science, and many offer advanced degrees. Curriculums for advanced degrees often emphasize a subfield such as microbiology or botany, but not all universities offer all curriculums. Advanced degree programs include classroom and field work, laboratory research, and a thesis or dissertation. Biological scientists who have advanced degrees often take temporary postdoctoral research positions that provide specialized research experience. In private industry, some biological scientists may become managers or administrators; others leave biology for nontechnical managerial, administrative, or sales jobs.

Biological scientists should be able to work equally efficiently on their own or as part of a team. In addition, they must be able to communicate clearly and concisely, both orally and in writing. Those in private industry who aspire to management or administrative positions should possess good business skills and be familiar with regulatory issues and marketing and management techniques. Those doing field research in remote areas must have physical stamina.

A Ph.D. degree in a biological science is the minimum education required for prospective medical scientists because the work of medical scientists is almost entirely research oriented. A Ph.D. degree qualifies one to do research on basic life processes or on particular medical problems or diseases, as well as analyze and interpret the results of experiments on patients. Medical scientists who administer drug or gene therapy to human patients or who otherwise interact medically with patients (such as drawing blood, excising tissue, or performing other invasive procedures) must have a medical degree. It is particularly helpful for medical scientists to earn both Ph.D. and medical degrees.

In addition to a formal education, medical scientists are usually expected to spend several years in a postdoctoral position before they are offered permanent jobs. Postdoctoral work provides valuable laboratory experience, including a background in specific processes and techniques (such as gene splicing) which are transferable to other research projects later on. In some institutions, the postdoctoral position can lead to a permanent position.

JOB OUTLOOK

Employment of biological and medical scientists is expected to increase faster than the average for all occupations through the year 2005. Nevertheless, job seekers can expect to face considerable competition for highly sought-after basic research positions. Biological and medical scientists will continue to conduct genetic and biotechnological research and help develop and produce products created by new biological methods. In addition, efforts to clean up and preserve the environment will continue to add to growth. More biological scientists will be needed to determine the environmental impact of industry and government actions and to correct past environmental problems. Expected expansion in research related to health issues such as AIDS, cancer, and the Human Genome Project should also result in growth. However, much research and development, including many areas of medical research, is funded by the federal government. Anticipated budget tightening should lead to smaller increases in research and development expenditures, further limiting the dollar amount of each grant and slowing the growth of the number of grants awarded to researchers. If, at the same time, the number of newly trained scientists continues to increase at a rate similar to that of the 1980s, both new and established scientists will experience greater difficulty winning and renewing research grants.

Persons with a bachelor's degree in biological science are usually not called biological scientists. Many find jobs as science or engineering technicians or health technologists and technicians. Some become high school biology teachers, and are regarded as teachers rather than biologists. Those with a doctorate in biological science may become college or university professors.

Biological and medical scientists are less likely to lose their jobs during recessions than those in many other occupations because most are employed on long-term research projects or in agricultural research. However, a recession could influence the amount of money allocated to new research and development efforts, particularly in areas of risky or innovative research. A recession could also limit the possibility of extension or renewal of existing projects.

SALARIES

Median annual earnings for biological and life scientists were about $37,500 in 1994; the middle 50 percent earned between $26,700 and $49,600. Ten percent earned less than $16,300, and 10 percent earned over $67,000. For medical scientists, median annual earnings were about $36,300; the middle 50 percent earned between $27,800 and $56,700. Ten percent earned less than $20,000, and 10 percent earned over $73,900.

According to the National Association of Colleges and Employers, beginning salary offers in private industry in 1995 averaged $22,900 a year for bachelor's degree recipients in biological science, about $29,400 for master's degree recipients, and about $48,000 for doctoral degree recipients.

In the federal government in 1995, general biological scientists in nonsupervisory, supervisory, and managerial positions earned an average salary of $48,290; microbiologists averaged $54,280; ecologists, $47,840; physiologists, $61,150; and geneticists, $60,110.

RELATED FIELDS

Many other occupations deal with living organisms and require a level of training similar to that of biological and medical scientists. These include the conservation occupations of forester, range manager, and soil conservationist, as well as animal breeders, horticulturists, soil scientists, and most other agricultural scientists. Many health professionals, including medical doctors, dentists, and veterinarians, also draw upon knowledge of the biological sciences.

INTERVIEW
Amadeo J. Pesce, Ph.D.
Professor of Experimental Medicine

Dr. Pesce serves as Director of the Toxicology Laboratory and Professor of Experimental Medicine at the University of Cincinnati Hospital. He has been associated with the University of Cincinnati for the past twenty-three years.

What the Job Is Really Like

"In most cases, I work as part of a team of researchers. The composition of the team may change depending on the project. Participants may include postdoctoral fellows, part-time or full-time technologists, pathologists, mathematicians, psychiatrists, substance abuse counselors, and other health and scientific professionals.

"Usually there are several projects going on at the same time. For instance, we're now helping with the clinical trials in developing methods of measurement for a couple of different projects. One project is to help pace patients by monitoring the effectiveness of the drug called AZT, which is used in the treatment of AIDS. We've developed the technology to measure the concentration of drugs inside the cell and are working very closely with the clinician and the clinical trials that are being conducted.

"Another project we're participating in is the study of developing agents that will help combat substance abuse by reducing the craving and the other aspects that make people want to continue to use drugs. In this project, we work with a group of psychiatrists and substance abuse counselors, and they provide specimens from the patients for us to monitor.

"In addition to the hours spent in the laboratory, a considerable portion of my time is spent thinking and writing. One must think things through and be able to communicate them effectively and efficiently in order for the research to have meaning. And, as I convey to my students, if it's not written down, it was never done.

"As an administrator, I have other responsibilities: I supervise a postdoctoral fellow and handle personnel issues and administrative problems. And, at this point in my life, I accomplish this and keep fairly regular working hours. But when I was younger (and for many years), I worked from seven in the morning until ten at night, five days a week. The other two days, I *only* worked eight to ten hours a day. This was not required, but just my own enthusiasm showing, based upon my decision to be one of the four most recognized authorities in the field. So I set on a path of learning all I could and then proceeded to put out a series of books (eighteen) about the field. This required an immense amount of work. I tell everyone that I did this to become rich and famous (my children always told me to skip the fame!), but, as it turns out, all I got was the fame. However, even though I didn't make the money I had hoped for, it has still been very rewarding. Fans as far away as Australia have asked me to sign their copies of my books.

"This career has many other rewards; uppermost is the accomplishment of developing a theory and finding supporting data. (After all, projects are funded grants for which you must show results by a certain date in order to be funded for the next project.) On the downside, the worst part of the job is when you write a paper, and it gets rejected by your peers (and you think they're wrong, and in fact you know they're wrong). However, the real issue for me is that we've done some pioneering work for people that has been fruitful and rewarding.

"Here's an example. A while back, we developed a way of looking at cancer in mice, and a colleague working on cancer research sent me a letter commending me on the work. The fact that somebody would think enough of our work to take what we've done and build on it is very rewarding.

"Another accomplishment relates to transplant patients. Some of the drugs used to treat these patients are very expensive, and we were able to devise a way of cutting the cost of those drugs from about $6,000 a year to about $1,200. This means that third world countries can actually afford the drug for their transplant patients. That's quite an accomplishment."

How Amadeo J. Pesce Got Started

"I always knew I was interested in medical research. So that's where I was focused early on. I earned my undergraduate degree at the Massachusetts Institute of Technology. Then I attended Brandeis University for my graduate degree in biochemistry. My postdoctoral scholarship was at the University of Illinois at Champaign–Urbana.

"To do this kind of work, you need to have Ph.D. credentials. I also have board certification from the American Board for Clinical Chemistry, which I think is very important. (Certification is given to those who have the proper scientific background, five years of experience in the field, and successful completion of an examination.)"

Expert Advice

"To be successful in this career, it helps to have an understanding partner, as I did. And since it is so important to be able to interact with people, exchange ideas, and get them to help with particular areas of your project, you must have the ability to get along with all kinds of people. You have to be aware of what issues others have and be able to accommodate them so they'll accommodate you in return. I have found that this is the proper approach to a successful collaboration. It's not unlike working with others on a book or any other project in which a number of people need to extend themselves in order to fulfill a common goal."

● ● ●

INTERVIEW
H. Graham Purchase, Ph.D.
Veterinary Medical Researcher

Dr. Purchase is Director of Veterinary Medical Research at Mississippi State University.

What the Job Is Really Like

"As a research administrator, my typical day here involves interacting with many individuals one-on-one. I handle the budget of the college, so often there are budget forms and various commitment forms to sign; for example, allowing individuals to travel, enabling people to buy new equipment, permitting staff to be hired. There are also manuscripts and proposals to review to make sure they're suitable. We are accredited by the American Association for the Accreditation of Laboratory Animal Care, and they have very high standards of review for all experiments on animals. Every single experiment that involves animals has to be reviewed by an animal-care-and-use committee to make sure that the animals are not harmed unnecessarily. Also, the accreditation involves making sure that the facilities are maintained, so that is another area of concern for me.

"A good part of my day is devoted to meetings with my superiors to inform them about how the research projects are progressing. Frequently, I have visitors to escort through our research facilities. I have reports to prepare on the research that we are doing, most of which are lay reports for general use for administrators and legislators. The actual writing of the research itself is done by the faculty. Our system is set up so that a designated faculty member will write the proposals, then the manuscripts will be sent out for peer review to make sure that the conclusions are supported by the data, and so on. I orchestrate that review process.

"We have many levels of researchers working here. Generally speaking, the principal investigators or leaders, the ones who actually design the experiments, have Ph.D.s. But we also have a variety of other types of careers involved. We have a lot of technicians; some have master's degrees, some have bachelor's degrees. We have animal caretakers and animal technicians; some of them have technician degrees, others are high school graduates. We have quite a number of students working toward bachelor's degrees who get some experience in the field by doing laboratory cleanup work here. Then we have graduate students and individuals who already have their bachelor's degrees who are going on to get their master's or Ph.D. degrees. These students spend a good deal of the time with their major professors learning how to conduct experiments and do research, so that when they graduate they'll know how to perform these tasks independently."

How H. Graham Purchase Got Started

"I was born in Rhodesia (now Zimbabwe), educated in Kenya, East Africa, and received my university training in South Africa. My father, also a veterinarian who worked in research, always said that since animals feed on plants, it's wise to learn about the plant world before going to veterinary school. So I went to college when I was sixteen and earned a bachelor's degree in botany. Following this, I completed my veterinary degree in South Africa, practiced for two years, and then fulfilled my dream of coming to the United States to do research. While employed here, I earned a master's and a Ph.D. at Michigan State University (majoring in microbiology and public health). It took eight years to complete my Ph.D., but it was well worth it.

"I started my research in a poultry laboratory in East Lansing, Michigan, and after a few years, met an American girl, married her, and decided to become a citizen of the United States. I worked at the poultry research laboratory performing research on tumor viruses of poultry species for about thirteen years. And this was one occasion where I can absolutely say that I was definitely at the right place at the right time, because the laboratory discovered the cause of one of the most economically devastating poultry diseases of the world (Market's disease, a form of cancer) and created a vaccine that would prevent the disease. The first commercially applicable cancer vaccine ever developed, it was initially patented and used in the United States extensively. Now it's used worldwide. This period was the most exciting and rewarding of my life.

"As a 'bench' researcher, I examined the cultures of cells in which we grew the disease-causing viruses or the vaccine that prevented the disease. Routinely, I would go to the necropsy room and find those birds that had died in the experiments. I would open the birds and examine what they died from to verify that it was the challenge and not something else unrelated to the experiment. The rest of the day would involve writing up manuscripts and grant proposals. Often writing was taken home to complete because many times I couldn't get it done during the daytime hours.

"After thirteen years, I moved up into administration and was offered a job in Washington, D.C. I spent fourteen years there, in nine different jobs in research administration. The research was in a variety of areas: plant, animal, human nutrition, family economics, soil, and water. But I have a great interest in veterinary research, and when the opportunity presented itself here at Mississippi State in the College of Veterinary Medicine, I took it. Here, we do research on the prime commodities of Mississippi, which include one of our big income producers—catfish—and our number one product—poultry."

Expert Advice

"If your grades are good, if you perform well during examinations, and if you can become an expert in these areas, research is a wonderful career. It's challenging and very innovative. I enjoy the ability to be able to develop something and to find out new things. But it's very rigorous, too. Most of my researchers are not here from nine to five. They're here early in the morning, they frequently miss their lunch breaks, and they take work home at night or come in at night and weekends to keep their work going. Research means pushing forward the frontiers of science, and, to succeed, you must be trained, prepared, and dedicated to putting in the necessary hours and effort."

● ● ●

INTERVIEW
Dennis J. Ernst
Clinical Microbiologist

Dennis J. Ernst is currently employed by the University of Louisville Hospital in Louisville, Kentucky. He is a medical technologist, certified by the American Society of Clinical Pathologists since 1978.

What the Job Is Really Like

"Medical technology involves the laboratory testing of body fluids and tissues for disease. This broad category consists of many subcategories. Through the years, I have worked them all in varying degrees but am currently engaged as a clinical microbiologist in a university hospital. I test blood, tissues, and body fluids for microorganisms that cause infection. I identify the microorganisms and suggest appropriate antibiotics to fight them. My work also includes immunology—the study of the presence of disease-fighting antibodies.

"I work four eight-hour days a week, enough to be considered a full-time employee. On a typical day, I begin by retrieving and collating data. This information is printed by an automated instrument that works throughout the night to identify microorganisms by species. This is obtained from patient cultures isolated the previous day. After identification, we determine the best antibiotic therapy against the particular organism. I enter the collated information into the hospital computer system and phone any life-threatening results to the appropriate physician for immediate treatment. Once reported, I set up newly isolated organisms for the same automated, overnight testing. Also, I am responsible for the maintenance of my automated equipment and for quality control processes that assure my analytical systems are functioning properly.

"The work has obvious risks since I can become infected by the very organisms that are infecting the patients whom I hope to help heal. However, with the proper and consistent use of personal protective devices such as gloves, gowns, and face shields, as well as implementing safe working habits, the risk is minimal. The work can be quite hectic when the hospital has many patients, but there are times when the patient population is low and the work is light. Often, there is not enough time in the day to complete all of my responsibilities. Since overtime is not allowed in our laboratory, any time spent working more than the hours scheduled must be offset by working proportionally less another day.

"Nearly all of my coworkers have either associate's or bachelor's degrees, and all are certified laboratory professionals in one capacity or another. The laboratory assistants who prepare the specimens for bacterial isolation and perform a multitude of nontechnical tasks are high school graduates who have received on-the-job training. The level of cooperation among us is high, as is our goal-oriented momentum. Rarely does a day pass when someone doesn't ask me if I need any help. This is the most satisfying aspect of my work."

How Dennis J. Ernst Got Started

"How I got started may be broken down into two parts: what attracted me to a career in the health sciences and what attracted me to a career as a medical technologist. The answers are completely different and say as much about the educational process as they do my impatience with it.

"My mother was a registered nurse whose feelings for caring for the sick inspired me back to my earliest recollection. Because of her dedication and the satisfaction she found in her work, I came to know that caring for the sick was a noble and rewarding thing. I saw her as someone who had been blessed by fate to see and know the inner workings of the human body, and for me to be so blessed when I came of age was an intriguing prospect.

"In high school, the sciences enhanced my interest in health care so much that upon graduation, I enrolled in the premed program at Albion College. My hopes were crushed the first week. My faculty advisor called me into his office two days after I had taken the science placement exams and said that my scores did not suggest that I was likely to succeed in the rigorous premed program. Further, he said that I was poorly prepared to major in any science curriculum whatsoever. I was stunned. If I couldn't major in the sciences, I didn't want to be on this or any other campus. Nothing else interested me. Too ignorant to take his advice and too stubborn to pursue another major, I defied his wisdom and vowed to prove him and the placement tests wrong. By the time I was a junior, I had proved them only half wrong. I was majoring in biology but pulling down only mediocre grades, far below what I needed to be considered for medical school. Though the sciences continued to intrigue me, my grade-point average had eliminated not only medical school but most other high-profile careers as well. By now the struggle had been long and hard, and I was wearing thin on persistence. I had experienced enough of education but still needed to emerge with a face-saving career of some security. The allied health fields presented many offerings, but most required more postgraduate study than I had the will to endure. Then my advisor recommended medical technology, the study of blood and disease. It was perfect! I could get that inside peek at the inner workings of the human body that I still craved and with only one year of postgraduate study. I applied for internships and was accepted."

Expert Advice

"Anyone interested in a career in the allied health sciences should consider medical technology for the insights it offers into the inner workings of the human body. Here, I found the constant discovery of the body's beauty and complexity that I hungered for as the young, observant son of a nurse. The intrigue has never ceased. Applications of the skills learned in training are many and varied, rendering the possibility of job burnout in this career remote. However, because of the sweeping application of managed care strategies in health care today, medical technology as a career has changed from one of promised permanence to one that is, at best, a stepping stone to a more secure and respected calling."

●   ●   ●

FOR MORE INFORMATION

For information on careers in physiology, contact:

American Physiological Society, Membership Services Dept., 9650 Rockville Pike, Bethesda, MD 20814

For information on careers in biotechnology, contact:

Biotechnology Industry Organization, 1625 K St. N.W., Suite 1100, Washington, D. C. 20006

For information on careers in biochemistry, contact:

American Society for Biochemistry and Molecular Biology, 9650 Rockville Pike, Bethesda, MD 20814

For information on careers in botany, contact:

> Business Office, Botanical Society of America, 1725 Neil Ave., Columbus, OH 43210-1293

For information on careers in microbiology, contact:

> American Society for Microbiology, Office of Education and Training–Career Information, 1325 Massachusetts Ave. N.W., Washington, D.C. 20005

Information on federal job opportunities is available from local offices of state employment services or offices of the United States Office of Personnel Management, located in major metropolitan areas.

CHAPTER 2

Careers in the Agricultural Sciences

EDUCATION
B.A./B.S. required; postgraduate work may be required

$$$ SALARY
$22,000 to $62,000

OVERVIEW
Agricultural Scientists

The work of agricultural scientists plays an important part in maintaining and increasing the world's agricultural productivity. Agricultural scientists study farm crops and animals and develop ways of improving their quantity and quality. They look for ways to improve crop yield and quality with less labor, avenues to control pests and weeds more safely and effectively, and techniques to conserve soil and water. They research methods of converting raw agricultural commodities into attractive and healthy food products for consumers.

Agricultural science is closely related to biological science, and agricultural scientists use the principles of biology, chemistry, and other sciences to solve problems in agriculture. They often work with biological scientists on basic biological research, or they may concentrate on applying the technological advances to agriculture.

Many agricultural scientists work in basic or applied research and development. Others manage or administer research and development programs or manage marketing or production operations in companies that produce food products or agricultural chemicals, supplies, and machinery. Some agricultural scientists are consultants to business firms, private clients, or government agencies.

Depending on the agricultural scientist's area of specialization, the nature of the work performed varies.

FOOD SCIENTISTS Food scientists or technologists are usually employed in the food processing industry, universities, or the federal government and help meet consumer demand for food products that are healthful, safe, palatable, and convenient. To do this, they use their knowledge of chemistry, microbiology, and other sciences to develop new or better ways of preserving, processing, packaging, storing, and delivering foods. Some engage in basic research: discovering new food sources; analyzing food content to determine levels of vitamins, fat, sugar, or protein; or searching for substitutes for harmful or undesirable additives such as nitrites. Many food technologists work in product development. Others enforce government regulations, inspecting food-processing areas and ensuring that sanitation, safety, quality, and waste-management standards are met.

PLANT SCIENTISTS Plant science encompasses the disciplines of agronomy, crop science, entomology, and plant breeding, among others. Plant scientists study plants and their growth in soils, helping producers of food, feed, and fiber crops to continue to feed a growing population while conserving natural resources and maintaining the environment. Agronomists and crop scientists not only help increase productivity but also study ways to improve the nutritional value of crops and the quality of seed. Some crop scientists study the breeding, physiology, and management of crops and use genetic engineering to develop crops resistant to pests and drought.

SOIL SCIENTISTS Soil scientists study the chemical, physical, biological, and mineralogical composition of soils as they relate to plant or crop growth. They study the responses of various soil types to fertilizers, tillage practices, and crop rotation. Many soil scientists who work for the federal government conduct soil surveys, classifying and mapping soils. They provide information and recommendations to farmers and other landowners regarding the best use of land and how to avoid or correct problems such as erosion. They may also consult with engineers and other technical personnel working on construction projects about the effects of and solutions to soil problems. Since soil science is closely related to environmental science, persons trained in soil science also apply their knowledge to ensure environmental quality and effective land use.

ANIMAL SCIENTISTS Animal scientists develop better, more efficient ways of producing and processing meat, poultry, eggs, and milk. Dairy scientists, poultry scientists, animal breeders, and other related scientists study the genetics, nutrition, reproduction, growth, and development of domestic farm animals. Some animal scientists inspect and grade livestock or food products, purchase livestock, or work in technical sales or marketing. As county extension agents or consultants, animal scientists advise agricultural producers on how to upgrade animal housing facilities properly, lower mortality rates, or increase production of animal products such as milk or eggs.

An entomologist talks to farmers about insect problems in growing corn and other crops.

TRAINING

Training requirements for agricultural scientists depend on the specialty and the type of work they perform. A bachelor's degree in agricultural science is sufficient for some jobs in applied research or in assisting in basic research, but a master's or doctoral degree is required for basic research. A Ph.D. degree in agricultural science is usually needed for college or university teaching and for advancement to administrative research positions. Degrees in related sciences such as biology, chemistry, or physics or in related engineering specialties also may qualify persons for some agricultural science jobs.

All states have land-grant colleges that offer agricultural science degrees. Many other colleges and universities also offer agricultural science degrees or some agricultural science courses. However, not every school offers all specialties. A typical undergraduate agricultural science curriculum includes communications, economics, business, and physical and life sciences courses, in addition to a wide variety of technical agricultural science courses. For prospective animal scientists, these technical agricultural science courses might include animal breeding, reproductive physiology, nutrition, and meats and muscle biology. Students preparing to become food scientists take courses in food chemistry, food analysis, food microbiology, and food processing operations. Those preparing to be crop or soil scientists take courses in plant pathology, soil chemistry, entomology, plant physiology, and biochemistry, among others. Advanced degree programs include classroom and fieldwork, laboratory research, and a thesis based on independent research.

Agricultural scientists should be able to work independently or as part of a team and be able to communicate clearly and concisely, both orally and in writing. Most agricultural scientists also need an understanding of basic business principles.

Agricultural scientists who have advanced degrees usually begin in research or teaching. With experience, they may advance to jobs such as supervisors of research programs or managers of other agriculture-related activities.

JOB OUTLOOK

Employment of agricultural scientists is expected to grow about as fast as the average for all occupations through the year 2005. Additionally, the need to replace agricultural scientists who retire or otherwise leave the occupation permanently will account for many more job openings than projected growth. Although the number of degrees awarded in agricultural science programs has been steady or even declined since the 1980s, new entrants, even those with advanced degrees, may still face competition for jobs as agricultural scientists. Animal and plant scientists with a background in molecular biology, microbiology, genetics, or biotechnology, soil scientists with an interest in the environment, and food technologists may find the best opportunities.

Generally speaking, those with advanced degrees will be in the best position to enter jobs as agricultural scientists.

However, competition for teaching positions in colleges or universities and for some basic research jobs may be keen, even for doctorate holders. Federal and state budget cuts may limit funding for these positions through the year 2005.

Bachelor's degree holders can work in some applied research and product development positions but usually only in certain subfields such as food science and technology. Also, the federal government hires bachelor's degree holders to work as soil scientists. Despite the more limited opportunities for those with only a bachelor's degree to obtain jobs as agricultural scientists, a bachelor's degree in agricultural science is useful for managerial jobs in businesses that deal with ranchers and farmers such as feed, fertilizer, seed, and farm equipment manufacturers, retailers or wholesalers, and farm credit institutions. Four-year degrees may also help persons seeking occupations such as cooperative extension service agents, farmers or farm or ranch managers, agricultural products inspectors, technicians, landscape architects, or purchasing or sales agents of agricultural commodities or farm supplies.

SALARIES

According to the National Association of Colleges and Employers, beginning salary offers in 1995 for graduates with a bachelor's degree in animal science averaged about $24,200 a year, and for graduates in plant science, $22,500.

Average federal salaries for employees in nonsupervisory, supervisory, and managerial positions in certain agricultural science specialties in 1995 were as follows: animal science, $61,480; agronomy, $49,270; soil science, $46,140; horticulture, $48,210; and entomology, $58,200.

RELATED FIELDS

The work of agricultural scientists is closely related to that of biologists and other natural scientists such as chemists, foresters, and conservation scientists. It is also related to agricultural production occupations such as farmer, farm manager, and cooperative extension service agent. Certain specialties of agricultural science are also related to other occupations. For example, the work of animal scientists is related to that of veterinarians. Horticulturists perform work that is similar to that of landscape architects, and soil scientists accomplish tasks that are similar to the work of soil conservationists.

INTERVIEW
Carl. I. Evensen, Ph.D.
Assistant Extension Specialist

Dr. Evensen serves as Assistant Extension Specialist for Natural Resource Management and Environmental Quality in the Department of Agronomy and Soil Science at the University of Hawaii.

What the Job Is Really Like

"My current job is extremely variable. Most of my time is spent on extension related activities, which involve planning training for extension agents (the faculty in the field who work most closely with farmers), speaking at and attending meetings with other government agencies and private industry, conducting teacher training, and making presentations at public events. Every day is different and holds its own challenges and rewards. I also seek grant funding and have led five projects in the last four years, mostly dealing with demonstrations of soil conservation, pesticide reduction, and education on pollution control. Of course, there are also administration and reporting requirements with all of these activities.

"Some days are spent entirely in my office either on the phone or at my computer, writing reports, summarizing data, responding to E-mail or correspondence. Other days (my favorites) are spent entirely in the field, teaching or collecting data in a field project. Usually, several days a month are spent traveling to neighboring islands to meet with agents and farmers or to participate in training. It also seems that I spend an inordinate amount of time (at least several hours or sometimes several days a week) in various meetings, either at the university or with various interagency groups.

"I also teach two graduate classes (Agriculture and the Environment, and Sustainable Agriculture) and am developing a new undergraduate course—Environmental Issues. Before teaching, I spend weeks selecting readings and discussion topics and planning the course syllabus. While teaching, I review the materials before class and try to keep up with current related topics to bring up in class. I also am a committee member on generally six to eight graduate student committees at any one time. Therefore, I also have scheduled and frequently unscheduled meetings with the students to discuss their projects. A great deal of time is also required for preparing and grading comprehensive exams, reading and commenting on students' theses or dissertations, and then participating in the final defense.

"I really enjoy the variety of activities and many new challenges I face every day. Teaching and working with graduate students is among the most enjoyable and challenging things that I do. However, I also really enjoy getting out in the field to work on a project or to work with farmers and agents. My less enjoyable responsibilities include reporting and project administration. Also, I sometimes get overwhelmed when a number of planned activities and unplanned requests or requirements coincide."

How Carl I. Evensen Got Started

"All my life, I have enjoyed gardening and growing crops, so the decision to go into agriculture as a profession seemed very natural to me. I also like working with other people and have found that I truly enjoy agricultural extension work, since it combines these interests and inclinations.

"After I earned my bachelor's degree in biology from Whitman College in Walla Walla, Washington, I was still very unsure of what I wanted to do as a profession. I decided that to give myself some time to think and to try to give back something to other people, I would join the Peace Corps. So I spent two years in Kenya working as a horticultural extensionist in an isolated part of the Coast Province called the Taita Hills. This was a wonderful, life-changing experience which convinced me that I wanted to work in agriculture but also pointed out the gaps in my knowledge.

"I then determined that I would go back to school to study agriculture and decided on the strong tropical agriculture program at the University of Hawaii. My master's program was spent studying agroforestry in Hawaii, while my Ph.D. research was performed in Indonesia, working on a soil management project. These studies gave me a strong background in soil fertility and crop nutrition, which I continue to use in my current job. Also, these overseas work experiences really broadened my perspective and helped me tremendously in understanding the needs of foreign graduate students. My subsequent job as an agronomist (1989–93) at the Hawaii Sugar Planters' Association (HSPA) was very valuable in giving me experience with large-scale plantation agriculture, as a contrast to my previous work with small-scale subsistence farmers. Also at HSPA, I began to work with soil and water conservation issues and problems."

Expert Advice

"I feel this type of job is very rewarding but also overwhelming and all-consuming. It is important to be organized and frequently reprioritize the multiple and changing activities so that the really critical things get done in a timely manner. However, it is also very important to avoid becoming consumed by the job. You must make time for yourself and your family in order to avoid becoming burned out."

●   ●   ●

INTERVIEW
Michael Moore, Ph.D.
Taxonomist

Dr. Moore serves as Curator in the Plant Department at the University of Georgia.

What the Job Is Really Like

"The herbarium (plant museum) at the University of Georgia is the largest in the state of Georgia. We have just over 200,000 mounted specimens. My responsibilities as curator are to make sure that the collection is maintained and curated in a proper manner. Then, I also have research projects which take me out into the field. This past year, for instance, I was out in the field every other week between March and October. I enjoy the fact that I work both inside and out-of-doors.

"We curators also have a responsibility to respond to questions from the public. Additionally, we exchange specimens with other herbaria, loan plants, and handle plant identifications as they come in.

"Over the years, I have also taught some classes at the university."

How Michael Moore Got Started

"As an undergraduate at the University of Georgia, I was already interested in this field. So, I stayed on as a graduate student and earned my master's degree in 1985 and my Ph.D. in 1989. I was lucky enough to get a job at the university even before I finished school. I've been Curator of the Herbarium in the Plant Department of the University of Georgia for three years."

Expert Advice

"Taxonomists can do many things. But you should realize that a master's degree is usually required and a Ph.D. is preferred for those who wish to assume this career. If you wish to focus on academia, you can do research as well as teach. Then you would want a heavy background in molecular biology and similar course work. If you want to be more of a field botanist—that is, someone who does more or less what I do in herbaria—or work with a private company protecting endangered species, you would want to have more ornamental horticulture training.

"Most major universities do have herbaria. The number of curators they have will depend on how many specimens they house. For example, in very large herbaria there will be individual curators who will be responsible for certain species or categories of plants.

"There are a number of hot topics which require the services of professionals in this field: conservation of the rain forest and environmental issues, for example. In the future, I think there will still be jobs for those who have a good basic background in taxonomy and are able to do basic field research."

• • •

INTERVIEW
Art Davis, Ph.D.
Cereal Chemist

Dr. Davis is the Director of Scientific Services at the American Association of Cereal Chemists, where he has served for the past two years.

What the Job Is Really Like

"Here at the American Association of Cereal Chemists, the main thing we do is offer about thirty short courses and other continuing education programs. Whenever there's a need to provide basic information in food science, we fill that void. For instance, there has been a tremendous growth in the use of frozen foods in this country in the last six or seven years, and a lot of (particularly smaller) companies are interested in getting into that field. Since there was no training available, we went out and found some people who were knowledgeable about this topic and put together a two-day course that provides the basics for those who need this information.

"Other courses we offer include water activity, wet milling sensory analysis, food technology, batter and breading technology, chemical leavening, breakfast cereal technology, chemistry technology, and principles of cereal science. Individuals often come to us with biology, microbiology, or engineering backgrounds but no experience with food technology. So, for individuals both overseas and here in the states, our courses provide the information needed.

"Another service we provide is an international check sample service. Monthly, bimonthly, or quarterly samples are sent to participating laboratories; specific analysis is performed, and the results are sent to us. We then compile all of the results and provide a report that reveals the status of perhaps a hundred laboratories. This gives the labs some idea of whether or not they are in line with other labs and how accurate their findings are. In fact, this year we're starting to do some proficiency certification. If you send all of the samples in for a year and your results are in line with the other labs, we'll issue you a certificate verifying that fact.

"Because there's a critical size that must be reached before it is feasible to establish your own research and development group, smaller companies tend to depend on their suppliers to do their research and development for them. For instance, my experience at the General Foods Bakeries taught me that you can make doughnut batter, starting with flour, sugar, salt, and so forth. But because of some of the peculiarities of putting doughnut ingredients together, it's a lot more efficient to buy a mix from a company that makes doughnut mixes. If you've got a problem with it, you can ask them to solve it, or if you want something a little bit different, you can ask them to create that for you. Flavor houses, mix suppliers, and fats and oils suppliers have their own research and development divisions, as do some of the bakers and mills. These are the people who can get you the properties you want. Thus, they'll go into their labs and massage the molecules until they come up with what you are looking for."

How Art Davis Got Started

"I obtained my bachelor's degree from Oregon State University and spent two years in the Peace Corps. Then, I went on to graduate school at Kansas State University, where I earned a master's and a Ph.D. in cereal chemistry. I knew I was always headed into biology and the sciences.

"After working for Pillsbury Company in their research and development department, I assumed a position heading a research group for the American Institute of Baking for about two and one-half years. Following that, I served on the faculty of Kansas State University for nine years. Subsequent positions included quality assurance manager for General Foods Bakeries and three years as the director of technical services for the Green Giant Fresh Vegetables Group."

Expert Advice

"For those interested in getting into food science, I would highly recommend Kansas State University's Department of Grain Science and Industry. They've got three curricula there: milling, baking, and seed plants (which has to do with building animal feeds). The undergraduate program, which includes serious chemistry, physics, and a little bit of engineering, is so excellent that every student who graduates from there has at least a couple of job offers. There is also a graduate program, and they never have any trouble placing those people either.

"Minnesota has a small but growing program in the cereals area through their food science department. Iowa State has a little bit through its Department of Food Science and Human Nutrition. Texas A & M has a couple of people who do pretty good work. It's not labeled food science there; I think it's called crop and food science. At the graduate level, Kansas State and North Dakota State University have good graduate programs, and A & M's got a graduate group that works in cereals, as does Iowa State. Just drop a line to those universities and see if their programs are of interest to you.

"If you are planning on doing research at a university, I'd recommend that you get a Ph.D. However, industry doesn't get terribly 'hung up' on degrees. I know a number of good researchers with master's degrees who have gone on and done quite well. I even know of a few with bachelor's degrees who have distinguished themselves. If you are an able researcher, there are opportunities out there for you."

● ● ●

INTERVIEW
Brent Steven Sipes, Ph.D.
Assistant Plant Pathologist

Dr. Sipes is employed by the University of Hawaii's Department of Plant Pathology in Honolulu, Hawaii. He came to the university as a junior researcher in 1991 to evaluate pineapple for resistance or tolerance to a plant parasite.

What the Job Is Really Like

"As an assistant professor, my days can vary greatly. Some days are spent indoors moving from one committee meeting to the next. Other days I spend at my desk analyzing and preparing data for presentations. Perhaps the best days are those when I am outside in the field collecting samples, setting up a test, or treating an experiment. Some days, I get to travel to experiments on neighboring islands. I even attend scientific meetings held all over the world.

"I have a great deal of flexibility as to the order of my day. I like to start early while the day is cool, around 7:00 A.M., and finish before it gets really hot, by 3:30 or 4:00 P.M., even if I am inside all day. Because 60 percent of my work involves field experiments, much of the work depends upon the weather. Rain can really ruin our best plans. Consequently, sometimes the work is very slow and easy, whereas other times everything needs to be done and there is hardly any time to take a breath.

"I work between forty-eight and fifty hours per week. Since I enjoy my job, I usually don't keep track of the hours. I work with many different types of people—senior professors and administrators, technical staff that assist me in my research, and students. Each group is different, and the challenge is to work well with everyone. The people in my laboratory are much like a family. We get along well together, although we may not always share the same opinions.

"What I like most about my work is the ability to pose questions and contemplate how to answer them. I like the freedom to choose my own path. I like to analyze data to answer those questions. I am honored by the respect my work affords me in the community."

How Brent Steven Sipes Got Started

"I very much enjoy the outdoors and plants. As a child, I was encouraged to garden by my next-door neighbor, a grandmotherly teacher. This interest in plants and their biology, systematics, and cultivation has followed me ever since.

"Majoring in plant pathology, I received my bachelor of science degree from Purdue University in West Lafayette, Indiana, in 1983. With the same specialty, I earned my M.S. and Ph.D. from North Carolina State University in Raleigh, North Carolina, in 1987 and 1991, respectively.

"Growing up in the sixties and seventies, I was also very conscientious of environmental stewardship. This activism motivated me to help in the proper use of pesticides to avoid problems which seemed to plague agricultural production. Becoming a plant pathologist, someone who studies plant diseases and their control, was a natural outgrowth.

"My first job was in a commercial greenhouse in Louisville, Kentucky. We grew roses which were shipped all over the Midwest. We had to regularly treat the plants with chemicals to ensure acceptable qualities and maintain production. This was a fun job but physically exhausting, and it taught me that I didn't want to be a common laborer the rest of my life.

"I spent three college summers working in a premier institution, the Morton Arboretum, located in a suburb of Chicago. Here, I was tutored by professional horticulturists who cared about plants and their well being. These people instilled within me the desire to perform quality work which would ensure that future generations would enjoy the plants in the collections of the arboretum. I learned much about plant classification—what made a rose a rose and a maple a maple (rather than an oak).

"I did well in college and knew before graduation that I would pursue an advanced degree. Graduate school agreed with me. I enjoyed the thrill of collecting and analyzing data from experiments, and from formulating and asking questions. I enjoyed conducting research."

Expert Advice

"If you are interested in and excited by this career, then commit yourself to it. The most important aspect to living is to enjoy your livelihood. Do not work to live on the weekends."

●　　●　　●

FOR MORE INFORMATION

Information on careers in agricultural science is available from:

> American Society of Agronomy, Crop Science Society of America, Soil Science Society of America, 677 S. Segoe Rd., Madison, WI 53711

> Food and Agricultural Careers for Tomorrow, Attn.: Dr. Allan Goecker, Purdue University, 1140 Agricultural Administration Bldg., West Lafayette, IN 47907-1140

For information on careers in food technology, write to:

> Institute of Food Technologists, Attn.: Dean Duxbury, Suite 300, 221 N. LaSalle St., Chicago IL 60601

For information on careers in animal science, write to:

> The American Society of Animal Science, 309 West Clark St., Champaign, IL 61820

Information on federal job opportunities is available from local offices of state employment security agencies or offices of the United States Office of Personnel Management, located in major metropolitan areas.

CHAPTER 3 Careers in the Physical Sciences

EDUCATION
B.A./B.S. required; Ph.D. may
be required

$$$ SALARY
$29,000 to $66,000

OVERVIEW
Chemists

Chemists search for and put to practical use new knowledge about chemicals. Although chemicals are often thought of as artificial or toxic substances, all physical things, whether naturally occurring or of human design, are composed of chemicals. Chemists have developed a tremendous variety of new and improved synthetic fibers, paints, adhesives, drugs, cosmetics, electronic components, lubricants, and thousands of other products. They also develop processes that save energy and reduce pollution such as improved oil refining and petrochemical processing methods. Research on the chemistry of living things spurs advances in medicine, agriculture, food processing, and other areas.

Many chemists work in research and development. In basic research, chemists investigate the properties, composition, and structure of matter and the laws that govern the combination of elements and reactions of substances. In applied research and development, chemists create new products and processes or improve existing ones, often using knowledge gained from basic research. For example, synthetic rubber and plastics resulted from research on small molecules uniting to form large ones (polymerization).

Chemists also work in production and quality control in chemical manufacturing plants. They prepare instructions for plant workers that specify ingredients, mixing times, and temperatures for each stage in the process. They also monitor automated processes to ensure proper product yield, and they test samples to ensure that they meet industry and government standards. Chemists also record and report on test results. Others are marketing or sales representatives who sell and provide technical information on chemical products.

Chemists often specialize in a subfield. Analytical chemists determine the structure, composition, and nature of substances and develop analytical techniques. They also identify the presence and concentration of chemical pollutants in air, water, and soil. Organic chemists study the chemistry of the vast number of carbon compounds. Many commercial products such as drugs, plastics, and fertilizers have been developed by organic chemists. Inorganic chemists study compounds consisting mainly of elements other than carbon such as those in electronic components. Physical chemists study the physical characteristics of atoms and molecules and investigate how chemical reactions work. Their research may result in new and better energy sources.

Chemists who work in production and quality control test samples to ensure that product specifications are met.

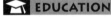

EDUCATION
Ph.D. required

$$$ SALARY
$45,000 to $77,000

Physicists and Astronomers

Physicists explore and identify basic principles governing the structure and behavior of matter, the generation and transfer of energy, and the interaction of matter and energy. Some physicists use these principles in theoretical areas such as the nature of time and the origin of the universe; others apply their physics knowledge to practical areas such as the development of advanced materials, electronic and optical devices, and medical equipment.

Physicists design and perform experiments with lasers, cyclotrons, telescopes, mass spectrometers, and other equipment. Based on observation and analysis, they attempt to discover laws that describe the forces of nature, such as gravity, electromagnetism, and nuclear interactions. They also find ways to apply physical laws and theories to problems in nuclear energy, electronics, optics, materials, communications, aerospace technology, navigation equipment, and medical instrumentation.

Most physicists work in research and development. Some do basic research to increase scientific knowledge. Physicists who conduct applied research build upon the discoveries made through basic research and work to develop new devices, products, and processes. For instance, basic research in solid-state physics led to the development of transistors and then to the integrated circuits used in computers.

Physicists also design research equipment. This equipment often has additional unanticipated uses. For example, lasers are used in surgery; microwave devices are used for ovens; and measuring instruments can analyze blood or the chemical content of foods. A small number work in inspection, testing, quality control, and other production-related jobs in industry.

Much physics research is done in small or medium-size laboratories. However, experiments in plasma, nuclear, high energy, and some other areas of physics require extremely large, expensive equipment such as particle accelerators. Physicists in these subfields often work in large teams. Although physics research may require extensive experimentation in laboratories, research physicists still spend time in offices planning, recording, analyzing, and reporting on research.

Physicists generally specialize in one of many subfields: elementary particle physics, nuclear physics, atomic and molecular physics, physics of condensed matter (solid-state physics), optics, acoustics, plasma physics, or the physics of fluids. Some specialize in a subdivision of one of these subfields; for example, within condensed matter physics, specialties include superconductivity, crystallography, and semiconductors. However, all physics involves the same fundamental principles, so specialties may overlap, and physicists may switch from one subfield to another. Also, growing numbers of physicists work in combined fields such as biophysics, chemical physics, and geophysics.

Astronomy is sometimes considered a subfield of physics. Astronomers use the principles of physics and mathematics to learn about the universe, including the sun, moon, planets, stars, and galaxies. They also apply their knowledge to problems in navigation and space flight.

Almost all astronomers do research. They analyze large quantities of data gathered by observatories and satellites and write scientific papers or reports on their findings. Most astronomers spend only a few weeks each year making observations with optical telescopes, radio telescopes, and other instruments. Contrary to the popular image, astronomers almost never make observations by looking directly through a telescope because enhanced photographic and electronic detecting equipment can see more than the human eye can.

Geologists and Geophysicists

EDUCATION
B.A./B.S. required; postgraduate work may be required

$$$ SALARY
$28,000 to $62,000

Geologists and geophysicists, also known as geological scientists or geoscientists, study the physical aspects and history of the earth. They identify and examine rocks, study information collected by remote sensing instruments in satellites, conduct geological surveys, construct maps, and use instruments to measure the earth's gravity and magnetic field. They also analyze information collected through seismic studies, which involves bouncing energy waves off buried rock layers. Many geologists and geophysicists search for oil, natural gas, minerals, and groundwater.

Other geological scientists play an important role in preserving and cleaning up the environment. Their activities include designing and monitoring waste disposal sites, preserving water supplies, reclaiming contaminated land and water, and ensuring compliance with federal environmental regulations. They also help locate safe sites for hazardous waste facilities and landfills.

Geologists and geophysicists examine chemical and physical properties of specimens in laboratories. They study fossil remains of animal and plant life or experiment with the flow of water and oil through rocks. Some geoscientists use two- or three-dimensional computer modeling to portray water layers and the flow of water or other fluids through rock cracks and porous materials. They use a variety of sophisticated laboratory instruments, including X-ray diffractometers, which determine the crystal structure of minerals, and petrographic microscopes for the study of rock and sediment samples. Geoscientists also use seismographs, instruments that measure energy waves resulting from movements in the earth's crust, to determine the locations and intensities of earthquakes.

Geoscientists working in the oil and gas industry sometimes process and interpret the maps produced by remote sensing satellites to help identify potential new oil or gas deposits. Seismic technology is also an important exploration tool. Seismic waves are used to develop three-dimensional computer models of underground or underwater rock formations.

Geologists and geophysicists also apply geological knowledge to engineering problems in constructing large buildings, dams, tunnels, and highways. Some administer and manage research and exploration programs; others become general managers in petroleum and mining companies.

Geology and geophysics are closely related fields, but there are major differences. Geologists study the composition, structure, and history of the earth's crust. They try to find out how rocks were formed and what has happened to them since their formation. Geophysicists use the principles of physics and mathematics to study not only the earth's surface but its internal composition, ground- and surface waters, atmosphere, and oceans, as well as its magnetic, electrical, and gravitational forces. Both scientists, however, commonly apply their skills to search for natural resources and solve environmental problems.

There are numerous subdisciplines or specialties that fall under the two major disciplines of geology and geophysics to further differentiate the kind of work geoscientists do. For example, petroleum geologists explore for oil and gas deposits by studying and mapping the subsurface of the ocean or land. They use sophisticated geophysical instrumentation, well log data, and computers to collect information. Mineralogists analyze and classify minerals and precious stones according to composition and structure. Paleontologists study fossils found in geological formations to trace the evolution of plant and animal life and the geologic history of the earth. Stratigraphers help to locate minerals by studying the distribution and arrangement of sedimentary rock layers and by examining the fossil and mineral content of such layers. Those who study marine geology are usually called oceanographers or marine geologists. They study and map the ocean floor and collect information using remote sensing devices aboard surface ships or underwater research craft.

Geophysicists may specialize in areas such as geodesy, seismology, or marine geophysics, also known as physical oceanography. Geodesists study the size and shape of the earth, its gravitational field, tides, polar motion, and rotation. Seismologists interpret data from seismographs and other geophysical instruments to detect earthquakes and locate earthquake-related faults. Physical oceanographers study the physical aspects of oceans such as currents and the interaction of sea surface and atmosphere.

Hydrology is a discipline closely related to geology and geophysics. Hydrologists study the distribution, circulation, and physical properties of underground and surface waters. They study the form and intensity of precipitation, its rate of infiltration into the soil, its movement through the earth, and its return to the ocean and atmosphere. The work they do is particularly important in environmental preservation and remediation.

☗ EDUCATION
B.A./B.S. required; postgraduate work may be required

$$$ SALARY
$22,000 to $50,000

Meteorologists

Meteorology is the study of the atmosphere, or the air that covers the earth. Meteorologists study the atmosphere's physical characteristics, motions, and processes, as well as the way it affects the rest of our environment. The best-known application of this knowledge is in forecasting the weather. However, weather information and meteorological research also are applied in air-pollution control, agriculture, air and sea transportation, defense, and the study of trends in the earth's climate such as global warming or ozone depletion.

Meteorologists who forecast the weather, known professionally as operational meteorologists, are the largest group of specialists in this field. They study information on air pressure, temperature, humidity, and wind velocity, and they apply physical and mathematical relationships to make short- and long-range weather forecasts. Their data comes from weather satellites, weather radar, remote sensors, and observers in many parts of the world. Meteorologists use sophisticated computer models of the world's atmosphere to make long-term, short-term, and local-area forecasts. These forecasts inform not only the general public but also those who need accurate weather information for both economic and safety reasons, as in the shipping, aviation, agriculture, fishing, and utilities industries.

The use of weather balloons, launched several times a day to measure wind, temperature, and humidity in the upper atmosphere, is supplemented by far more sophisticated weather equipment that transmits data as frequently as every few minutes. Doppler radar, for example, can detect rotational patterns in violent storm systems, allowing forecasters to better predict the occurrence of thunderstorms, tornadoes, and flash floods, as well as their direction and intensity.

Some meteorologists work in research. Physical meteorologists, for example, study the atmosphere's chemical and physical properties; the transmission of light, sound, and radio waves; and the transfer of energy in the atmosphere. They also study factors affecting the formation of clouds, rain, snow, storms, and other weather phenomena. Climatologists collect, analyze, and interpret past records of wind, rainfall, sunshine, and temperature in specific areas or regions. Their studies are used to design buildings, plan heating and cooling systems, and aid in effective land use and agricultural production. Other research meteorologists examine the most effective ways to control or diminish air pollution or improve weather forecasting using mathematical models.

Jobs in weather stations, most of which operate around the clock seven days a week, often involve night, weekend and holiday work, and rotating shifts. During times of weather emergencies such as hurricanes, operational meteorologists may work overtime. Operational meteorologists are also often under pressure to meet forecast deadlines. Weather stations are found all over the country: in airports, in or near cities, and in isolated and remote areas. Some meteorologists also spend time observing weather conditions and collecting data from aircraft. Meteorologists in smaller weather offices often work alone. Sometimes, those working in larger offices work as members of a team. Meteorologists not involved in forecasting work regular hours, usually in offices. Those who work for private consulting firms or for companies that analyze and monitor emissions to improve air quality often work with other science or engineering professionals.

TRAINING
Chemists

A bachelor's degree in chemistry or a related discipline is usually the minimum education necessary to work as a chemist. However, many, if not most, research jobs require a Ph.D. degree.

Many colleges and universities offer a bachelor's degree program in chemistry; over six hundred are approved by the American Chemical Society. Several hundred colleges and universities also offer advanced degree programs in chemistry.

Students planning careers as chemists should enjoy studying science and mathematics and like working with their hands building scientific apparatus and performing experiments. Perseverance, curiosity, and the ability to concentrate on detail and to work independently are essential. In addition to taking required courses in analytical, inorganic, organic, and physical chemistry, undergraduate chemistry majors usually study biological sciences, mathematics, and physics. Computer courses are invaluable, as employers increasingly prefer job applicants to be not only computer literate but able to apply computer skills to modeling and simulation tasks. Laboratory instruments are also computerized, and the ability to operate and understand equipment is essential.

Because research and development chemists are increasingly expected to work on interdisciplinary teams, some understanding of other disciplines, including business and marketing or economics, is desirable, along with leadership ability and good oral and written communication skills. Experience, either in academic laboratories or through internships or co-op programs in industry, also is useful. Some employers of research chemists, particularly in the pharmaceutical industry, prefer to hire individuals with several years of postdoctoral experience.

Although graduate students typically specialize in a sub-field of chemistry, such as analytical chemistry or polymer chemistry, students usually need not specialize at the under-graduate level. In fact, undergraduates who are broadly trained have more flexibility when job hunting or changing jobs than if they narrowly define their interests. Most employers provide new bachelor's degree chemists with additional training or education.

In government or industry, beginning chemists with a bachelor's degree work in technical sales or services, quality control, or assist senior chemists in research and development laboratories. Some may work in research positions, analyzing and testing products, but these may be technician positions with limited upward mobility. Many employers prefer chemists with a Ph.D. to work in basic and applied research. A Ph.D. is also generally preferred for advancement to many administrative positions. Chemists who work in sales, marketing, or professional research positions often eventually move into management.

Many people with a bachelor's degree in chemistry enter other occupations in which a chemistry background is helpful such as technical writing or chemical marketing. Some enter medical, dental, veterinary, or other health profession schools. Others choose from a wide range of occupations with little or no connection to chemistry.

Chemistry graduates may become high school teachers, and those with a Ph.D. may teach at the college or university level. However, they usually are then regarded as science teachers, or college or university faculty, rather than chemists. Others may qualify as engineers, especially if they have taken some courses in engineering.

Physicists and Astronomers

A doctoral degree is the usual educational requirement for physicists and astronomers because most jobs are in research and development. Many physics and astronomy Ph.D. holders ultimately take jobs teaching at the college or university level. Additional experience and training in a postdoctoral research assignment, although not required, is helpful in preparing physicists and astronomers for permanent research positions.

Those with only bachelor's or master's degrees in physics are rarely qualified to fill positions as physicists. They are, however, usually qualified to work in an engineering-related area or other scientific fields, to work as technicians, or to assist in setting up laboratories. Some may qualify for applied research jobs in private industry or nonresearch positions in the federal government, and a master's degree often suffices for teaching jobs in two-year colleges. Astronomy bachelor's degree holders often enter a field unrelated to astronomy, but they are also qualified to work in planetariums running science shows or to assist astronomers doing research.

Hundreds of colleges and universities offer bachelor's degrees in physics. The undergraduate program provides a broad background in the natural sciences and mathematics. Typical physics courses include mechanics, electromagnetism, optics, thermodynamics, atomic physics, and quantum mechanics.

About 180 colleges and universities have physics departments that offer Ph.D. degrees in physics. Graduate students usually concentrate in a subfield of physics such as elementary particles or condensed matter. Many begin studying for their doctorate immediately after earning their bachelor's degree.

About forty universities offer a Ph.D. degree in astronomy, either through an astronomy department, a physics department, or a combined physics/astronomy department. Applicants to astronomy doctoral programs face keen competition for available slots. Those planning a career in astronomy should have a very strong physics background. In fact, an undergraduate degree in physics is excellent preparation, followed by a Ph.D. in astronomy.

Mathematical ability, computer skills, an inquisitive mind, imagination, and the ability to work independently are important traits for anyone planning a career in physics or astronomy. Prospective physicists who hope to work in industrial laboratories applying physics knowledge to practical problems should broaden their educational background to include courses outside of physics such as economics, computer technology, and current affairs. Good oral and written communication skills are also important because many physicists work as part of a team or have contact with persons with nonphysics backgrounds such as clients or customers.

The beginning job for most Ph.D. physics and astronomy graduates is conducting research in a postdoctoral position, where they may work with experienced physicists as they continue to learn about their specialty and develop ideas and results to be used in later work. The initial work may be routine and under the close supervision of senior scientists. After gaining some experience, they perform more complex tasks and work more independently. Physicists who develop new products or processes sometimes form their own companies or join new firms to exploit their own ideas.

Geologists and Geophysicists

A bachelor's degree in geology or geophysics is adequate for entry into some lower level geology jobs, but better jobs with good advancement potential usually require at least a master's degree in geology or geophysics. Persons with strong backgrounds in physics, chemistry, mathematics, or computer science also may qualify for some geophysics or geology jobs. A Ph.D. degree is required for most research positions in colleges and universities and is also important for work in federal agencies and some state geological surveys that involve basic research.

Hundreds of colleges and universities offer bachelor's degree programs in geology, geophysics, oceanography, or other geosciences. Other programs offer related training for beginning geological scientists in areas such as geophysical technology, geophysical engineering, geophysical prospecting, engineering geology, petroleum geology, hydrology, and geochemistry. In addition, several hundred more universities award advanced degrees in geology or geophysics.

Geologists and geophysicists need to be able to work as part of a team. Computer modeling, data processing, and effective oral and written communication skills are important, as well as the ability to think independently and creatively. Those involved in fieldwork must have physical stamina.

Traditional geoscience courses emphasizing classical geologic methods and topics (such as mineralogy, paleontology, stratigraphy, and structural geology) are important for all geoscientists. However, those students interested in working in the environmental or regulatory fields should take courses in hydrology, hazardous waste management, environmental legislation, chemistry, mechanics, and geologic logging. Also, some employers seek applicants with field experience, so a summer internship or employment in an environmentally related area may be beneficial to prospective geoscientists.

Geologists and geophysicists often begin their careers in field exploration or as research assistants in laboratories. They are given more difficult assignments as they gain experience. Eventually, they may be promoted to project leader, program manager, or another management or research position.

Meteorologists

A bachelor's degree with a major in meteorology or a closely related field with course work in meteorology is the usual minimum requirement for a beginning job as a meteorologist.

The preferred educational requirement for entry level meteorologists in the federal government is a bachelor's degree, not necessarily in meteorology, with at least twenty semester hours of meteorology courses, including six hours in weather analysis and forecasting and six hours in dynamic meteorology. In addition to meteorology course work, differential and integral calculus and six hours of college physics are required for federal meteorology positions. These requirements have recently been upgraded to include course work in computer science and additional course work appropriate for a physical science major, including statistics, chemistry, physical oceanography, or physical climatology. Sometimes, a combination of experience and education may be substituted for a degree.

Although positions in operational meteorology are available for those with only a bachelor's degree, obtaining a graduate degree enhances advancement potential. A master's degree is usually necessary for conducting research and development, and a Ph.D. may be required for some research positions. Students who plan a career in research and development need not necessarily major in meteorology in undergraduate school. In fact, a bachelor's degree in mathematics, physics, or engineering is excellent preparation for graduate study in meteorology.

The federal government's National Weather Service is the largest employer of civilian meteorologists.

Because meteorology is a small field, relatively few colleges and universities offer degrees in meteorology or atmospheric science, although many departments of physics, earth science, geography, and geophysics offer atmospheric science and related courses. Prospective students should make certain that courses required by the National Weather Service and other employers are offered at the college or university they are considering. Computer science courses, additional meteorology courses, and a strong background in mathematics and physics are important to prospective employers. Many programs combine the study of meteorology with another field such as agriculture, engineering, or physics. For example, hydrometeorology is the blending of hydrology (the science of the earth's water) and meteorology, and is concerned with the effect of precipitation on the hydrologic cycle and the environment.

Beginning meteorologists often do routine data collection, computation, or analysis and some basic forecasting. Entry level meteorologists in the federal government are usually placed in intern positions for training and experience. Experienced meteorologists may advance to various supervisory or administrative jobs or may handle more complex forecasting jobs. Increasing numbers of meteorologists establish their own weather consulting services.

JOB OUTLOOK
Chemists

Employment of chemists is expected to grow about as fast as the average for all occupations through the year 2005. The chemical industry, the major employer of chemists, should face continued demand for goods such as new and better pharmaceuticals and personal care products, as well as more specialty chemicals designed to address specific problems or applications. To meet these demands, research and development expenditures in the chemical industry will continue to increase, contributing to employment opportunities for chemists.

Within the chemical industry, job opportunities are expected to be most plentiful in pharmaceutical and biotechnology firms. Stronger competition among drug companies and an aging population are among the several factors contributing to the need for innovative and improved drugs discovered through scientific research. Although employment growth is expected to be slower in the remaining segments of the chemical industry, there will still be a need for chemists to develop and improve products such as cosmetics and cleansers, as well as the technologies and processes used to produce chemicals for all purposes. Job growth will also be spurred by the need for chemists to monitor and measure air and water pollutants to ensure compliance with local, state, and federal environmental regulations.

Because much employment growth for chemists is expected to relate to drug research and development and environmental issues, analytical, environmental, and synthetic organic chemists should have the best job prospects.

During periods of economic recession, layoffs of chemists may occur, especially in the oil refining and industrial chemicals industries. Chemists are vulnerable to temporary slowdowns in automobile manufacturing and construction, the end users of many of the products of the chemical industry.

Physicists and Astronomers

A large proportion of physicists and astronomers are employed on research projects, many of which, in the past, were defense related. Expected reductions in defense-related research and an expected slowdown in the growth of civilian physics-related research will cause employment of physicists and astronomers to decline through the year 2005. Proposed employment cutbacks and overall budget tightening in the federal government will also affect employment of physicists, especially those dependent on federal research grants. The number of doctorates granted in physics has been much greater than the number of openings for physicists for several years. Although physics enrollments are starting to decline slightly, the number of new Ph.D. graduates is likely to continue to be high enough to result in keen competition for the kind of research and academic jobs that those with new doctorates in physics have traditionally sought. Also, more prospective researchers will likely compete for less grant money.

Although research and development budgets in private industry will continue to grow, many research laboratories in private industry are expected to reduce basic research, which is where much physics research takes place, in favor of applied or manufacturing research and product and software development. Furthermore, although the median age of physicists and astronomers is higher than the average for all occupations and many will be eligible for retirement in the next decade, it is possible that many of them will not be replaced when they retire.

Persons with only a bachelor's degree in physics or astronomy are not qualified to enter most physicist or astronomer jobs. However, many find jobs as high school physics teachers and in engineering, technician, mathematics, and computer and environment-related occupations. Despite the strong competition for and expected employment declines in traditional physics and astronomical research-oriented jobs, individuals with a physics degree at any level will find their skills useful for entry into many other occupations.

Geologists and Geophysicists

Many jobs for geologists and geophysicists are in or related to the petroleum industry, especially the exploration for oil and gas. This industry is subject to cyclical fluctuations. Low oil prices, higher production costs, improvements in energy efficiency, shrinking oil reserves, and restrictions on potential drilling sites have caused exploration activities to be curtailed in the United States. If these conditions continue, there will be limited openings in the petroleum industry for geoscientists working in the United States.

As a result of generally poor job prospects in the past few years, the number of students enrolling in geology and geophysics has dropped considerably. Although enrollments are rising again, the number of students trained in petroleum geology is likely to be so low that even a small increase in openings in the oil industry will be greater than the number of petroleum geologists and geophysicists available to fill them, creating good employment opportunities if exploration activities increase significantly. Employment prospects will be best for job seekers who hold a master's degree and are familiar with advanced technologies such as computer modeling, which are increasingly used to locate new oil and gas fields or pinpoint hidden deposits in existing fields. Because of the cyclical nature of the oil and gas industry, hiring on a contractual basis is common.

Despite the generally poor job prospects encountered by geoscientists in recent years in the petroleum industry, employment of geologists and geophysicists is expected to grow as fast as the average for all occupations through the year 2005. Recent setbacks have been offset by increased demand for these professionals in environmental protection and reclamation. Geologists and geophysicists will continue to be needed to help clean up contaminated sites in the United States, and to help private companies and government comply with more numerous and complex environmental regulations. In particular, jobs requiring training in engineering geology, hydrology, and geochemistry should be in demand. However, the number of geoscientists obtaining training in these areas has been increasing, so they may experience competition despite the increasing number of jobs available.

Meteorologists

Persons seeking employment as meteorologists are likely to face competition because the National Weather Service, the largest single employer of meteorologists, has curtailed hiring following an extensive modernization of its weather forecasting equipment. Employment of meteorologists is expected to grow more slowly than the average for all occupations through the year 2005. Employment of meteorologists in other parts of the federal government is not expected to increase either. Some employment growth is anticipated in private industry as the use of private weather forecasting and meteorological services by farmers, commodity investors, utilities, transportation and construction firms, and radio and television stations increases. For people in these and other areas, specific weather information more closely targeted to their needs than the general information provided by the National Weather Service can yield significant benefits. However, because many private weather service customers are in industries sensitive to fluctuations in the economy, the sales and growth of private weather services depend on the health of the economy.

There will continue to be demand for meteorologists to analyze and monitor the dispersion of pollutants into the air to ensure compliance with the federal environmental regulations outlined in the Clean Air Act of 1990.

SALARIES
Chemists

According to a 1995 survey by the National Association of Colleges and Employers, the average starting salary for recently graduated chemists with a bachelor's degree was about $29,300 a year; for those with a master's degree, it was $38,000; and for those with a Ph.D., it was $52,900.

A survey by the American Chemical Society reports that the median salary of all their members with a bachelor's degree was $45,400 a year in 1994; with a master's degree, it was $53,500; and with a Ph.D., it was $66,000.

In 1995, chemists in nonsupervisory, supervisory, and managerial positions in the federal government earned an average salary of $56,070.

Physicists and Astronomers

The American Institute of Physics reported a median salary of $64,000 in 1994 for its members with Ph.D.s. Those working in four-year colleges (nine or ten months a year) earned the least—$45,000, while those employed in industry and hospitals earned the most—$75,000 and $77,000, respectively.

Average earnings for physicists in nonsupervisory, supervisory, and managerial positions in the federal government in 1995 were $67,240 a year; and for astronomy and space scientists, the average was $71,660.

Geologists and Geophysicists

Surveys by the National Association of Colleges and Employers indicate that graduates with bachelor's degrees in geology and the geological sciences received an average starting offer of about $27,900 a year in 1995. However, the starting salaries can vary widely, depending on the employing industry. For example, according to a 1994 American Association of Petroleum Geologists survey, the average salary in the oil and gas industry for geoscientists with less than two years of experience was about $42,500.

Although the petroleum, mineral, and mining industries offer higher salaries, the competition in these areas is normally intense, and the job security is less than in other areas.

In 1995, the federal government's average salary for geologists in managerial, supervisory, and nonsupervisory positions was $55,540; geophysicists averaged $62,220; hydrologists averaged $51,080; and oceanographers averaged $58,980.

Meteorologists

According to an American Meteorological Society survey, the average entry level salary for meteorologists with a bachelor's degree was about $22,000 in 1992; for those with a master's degree, the average was $27,000; and for those with a Ph.D. degree, the average was $37,000.

The average salary for meteorologists in nonsupervisory, supervisory, and managerial positions in the federal government was $50,540 in 1995. In 1995, government-employed meteorologists with a bachelor's degree and no experience received a starting salary between $18,700 and $23,200 a year, depending on their college grades. Those with a master's degree started between $23,200 and $28,300; those with a Ph.D. degree started between $34,300 and $41,100. Beginning salaries for all degree levels were slightly higher in selected areas of the country where the prevailing local pay level was higher.

RELATED FIELDS

The work of chemical engineers, agricultural scientists, biological scientists, and chemical technicians is closely related to the work done by chemists. The work of other physical and life science occupations such as physicists and medical scientists may also be similar to that of chemists.

The work of physicists and astronomers relates closely to that of other scientific and mathematics occupations such as chemist, geologist, geophysicist, and mathematician. Engineers and engineering and science technicians also use the principles of physics in their work.

Many geologists and geophysicists work in the petroleum and natural gas industry. This industry also employs many other workers in the scientific and technical aspects of petroleum and natural gas exploration and extraction, in positions including engineering technicians, science technicians, petroleum engineers, and surveyors. Also, some life scientists, physicists, chemists, and meteorologists, as well as mathematicians, computer scientists, soil scientists, and mapping scientists, perform related work in both petroleum and natural gas exploration and extraction and in environment-related activities.

Workers in other occupations concerned with the physical environment include oceanographers; geologists and geophysicists; hydrologists; civil, chemical, and environmental engineers; physicists; and mathematicians.

INTERVIEW
Sara Sawtelle, Ph.D.
Manager of Technical Services

Dr. Sawtelle serves as Manager of Technical Services at Environmental Test Systems, Inc., in Elkhart, Indiana. Environmental Test Systems (ETS) was founded in 1985 to develop consumer and industrial applications for reagent strip technology. Test strips have been widely used in the medical diagnostic industry since the 1960s when their introduction revolutionized the way physicians performed urinalysis and blood tests. The company has adapted the technology for applications in such diverse fields as pool and spa water testing, drinking-water quality testing, automobile and diesel truck coolant testing, and industrial in-process testing. Research and development efforts are ongoing as scientists continuously explore a variety of potential applications for the test strip.

What the Job Is Really Like

"My job does not have a typical day. I am very busy but not overstressed. I work forty-plus hours per week in an atmosphere that is very team oriented. As a member of technical services, I am a part of the marketing department. This enables me to share the joy of chemistry with others, particularly nonchemists. I find the interactions intriguing and usually come away learning more all the time. It is also an environment that encourages 'out of the box' thinking, one in which we are encouraged to grow and learn. I assist customers with technical questions, acting as the technical liaison between the lab and the marketing department. I spend time talking with customers about our products, learn about new products that are coming out, and help in the leg work of marketing and developing a new product.

"I really enjoy working in this environment. The strength of this company is that, from the president down to the line worker, everyone is considered important and has an invaluable function. It is a nice atmosphere in which to thrive.

"The most difficult part of the job is working with difficult customers. But this is to be expected. Still, the hard part is not letting them get to you so that you join them in their attitude.

"Most of my job centers around communication—communication within the company—communication between scientists and nonscientists, communication externally with customers and explaining 'problems' to them in lay terms. Communication is also of the utmost importance to presentations which are given to professionals in the fields that use our products.

"My previous experience of five years of teaching chemistry at the college level has been very valuable in this undertaking. Among other things, it taught me how to listen and not jump to conclusions about what a person may be asking."

How Sara Sawtelle Got Started

"I was attracted to chemistry because of all the interesting things that are part of chemistry. The more I learned, the more intrigued I became with how chemistry and life were connected. So, I pursued an education focused in science.

"I earned my bachelor's degree in science (with a major in chemistry) from Clarion University in Pennsylvania, in 1988. Subsequently, I earned my Ph.D. in analytical chemistry from Boston College in Chestnut Hill, Massachusetts, in 1992.

"I started here on May 12, 1997. Environmental Test Systems was looking for a chemist with good communication and people skills. At the time, I was teaching at a local college while seeking an area position that would let me make use of the parts of teaching that I enjoy, while omitting the parts I did not. This position does just that!"

Expert Advice

"My advice is to believe in yourself and not try to be someone else. Don't try to change who you are. And don't expect that the first job you get out of college or school to be 'the job' for you. As you grow as a person, be willing to try new things or new career paths. I never thought I would be where I am. I expected to become a college professor. But once I tried teaching, I found that there were aspects of the profession that did not work for me. I like being in the position I am. So, I guess my advice is to make sure you like your career—or it is just not worth your energy. If you don't like it, move on."

● ● ●

INTERVIEW
Ken Rubin, Ph.D.
Assistant Professor

Dr. Rubin serves on the staff of the University of Hawaii in the Department of Geology and Geophysics, School of Ocean and Earth Science and Technology (SOEST).

What the Job Is Really Like

"I work seven days a week, between eight and twelve hours a day. Part of this may be because I am not yet tenured, and part of it is because my particular brand of research requires lengthy and exacting analytical procedures in a clean room environment that makes progress slow unless you put in long hours. But part of why I work so much is simply because I enjoy it and have taken on other nonresearch and nonteaching duties as 'extras.'

"I teach one or two upper-division and/or graduate level classroom courses per semester and presently am advising three graduate students (two doctoral, one M.S.). I do my lab research in one- to two-month chunks where I may spend all my nonclassroom time in the lab, or in the field (both on ocean-going research vessels and on land), or in my office reducing data and interpreting results.

"Some of my fieldwork, which includes research on active volcanoes on land and on the sea floor is 'dangerous,' and almost all of my lab work involves toxic chemicals and radioactive substances. This work isn't for everyone, but I find it rewarding because of the day-to-day challenges. The part that makes it unique, and the difficult thing to pass on to students, is the application of high-precision measurements requiring exacting care and uncompromising standards to natural phenomena. Although the lab and fieldwork are both necessary aspects of the research we do, the two environments are very different and require different mind-sets.

"In addition to these things, I have also worked to get our school (SOEST) and its departments, students, and faculty on-line to the Internet. I developed and oversee numerous web sites at our school, including interactive sites providing answers to the public for questions about science, and resource sites dedicated to educating lay people and researchers about active processes at volcanoes and the latest research going on at the University of Hawaii. I use the Internet in my courses and love what it offers. Once people relate to and accept the way in which computers process and make information available, their minds are freed to cross the boundaries between the abstract and the physical. Computers are a wonderful and indispensable teaching tool.

"There are, of course, many trade-offs with this sort of job. To enjoy the academic and intellectual freedom, friendly atmosphere, youthful environment, and flexible hours, one must be very disciplined. This can make it difficult, as you must evaluate yourself and your progress frequently and cannot rely on infrequent or nonexistent direction from a superior. You must 'sense' the expectations of your peers and then work to satisfy them while not sacrificing your own goals and desires. You must be self-motivated and take a very long-range perspective on success in the attainment of work-related goals.

"Additionally, today's academic scientist must deal with lack of funds at all levels. The golden age of scientific research died out in the 1980s (if not earlier). I watch my older colleagues struggling to adapt to this new environment, but since I never knew the days of seemingly unlimited research funds, I don't get as depressed as they at the difficulty of getting research funded today."

How Ken Rubin Got Started

"I earned my B.A. from the University of California (San Diego) in chemistry in 1984. Following this, I pursued my graduate training at the University of California (San Diego) Scripps Institute of Oceanography and received my M.S. in 1985 and my Ph.D. in 1991. I came to the University of Hawaii in February of 1992 as an assistant researcher and became an assistant professor in January of 1995.

"Essentially, I was hired at the University of Hawaii right out of graduate school (although I spent about nine months doing postdoctorate work at Scripps Institute of Oceanography before actually starting my job at UH). I was hired in a competitive search for a postdoctorate position known as the SOEST Young Investigator. This position is better than a simple postdoctorate in that it is actually a research faculty position (at the assistant level) that allows one to write grant proposals to federal funding agencies and to work independent of a supervisor. The School of Ocean and Earth Science and Technology (SOEST) offers one or two of these positions a year, with applicants being chosen from a variety of disciplines (earth sciences, oceanography, marine biology, atmospheric sciences, ocean engineering). Other universities offer these sorts of 'institutional' postdoctorate positions with varying levels of support and duration.

"Once at the University of Hawaii, I entered into an agreement with our school's dean and other faculty to set up a state-of-the-art thermal ionization mass spectrometry facility for analyzing radioactive isotopes. This was a serious commitment for all involved because the time frame for getting a lab of this sort funded and up and running is three to five years, longer than the two-year position I was given. However, I was given verbal agreement that, pending significant productivity on my part, my assistant researcher position could be extended beyond the original two-year period.

"At the time (1992), there were only two other facilities of this type in the country (outside of restricted-access national laboratories). Now, there are probably five or so. Setting up the lab required getting federal support for the purchase of a $750,000 mass spectrometer. I funded it with 25 percent each from the National Science Foundation Earth Sciences and Ocean Sciences Divisions and 50 percent from SOEST.

"After successfully getting the instrument funded and starting to get the laboratory set up, I was offered an assistant professor position at the University of Miami's Rosenstiel School of Marine and Atmospheric Sciences (RSMAS). At the time (spring, 1994), the state of Hawaii was just entering an economic downturn, and I felt it was necessary to encourage the university into making our relationship more 'formal' by getting a solid offer from another institution. I would have been willing to move to another locale but preferred to continue here at UH. Following this, an assistant professor position was approved by SOEST and UH, a national search was conducted, and I was chosen for the position. So, here I am.

"I started undergraduate school wanting to be a medical doctor. But, during my freshman year, I became really turned on to chemistry with environmental applications. Simultaneously, I fell in love with the academician's career and lifestyle. I immediately changed my career aspirations to becoming a professor at a research university. I have nothing against private sector or government jobs, and know I could find some level of fulfillment in pursuits there. However, it was clear to me then and still is today that the level of intellectual freedom that the university system in America affords makes this sort of job highly rewarding."

Expert Advice

"Jobs are very difficult to obtain, so always work hard at everything you do. Not only are top-notch resumes required to land one of these jobs, but hard work will be required to keep it. A university professor's life may appear to be genteel and rewarding and filled with healthy doses of wisdom and cups of cappuccino at the local coffee house, but it is actually rigorous on many levels."

● ● ●

INTERVIEW
Kevin T. M. Johnson, Ph.D.
Research Geologist

Dr. Johnson is employed by both the Bishop Museum and the University of Hawaii in Honolulu, Hawaii.

What the Job Is Really Like

"My job is quite varied. I spend about 75 to 80 percent of my time doing basic marine geological research on projects that I have received external funding to carry out. Most of my research funding is from the National Science Foundation. Primarily, my projects deal with the formation of ocean basins and oceanic crust at midocean ridges and oceanic islands. I spend months at sea each year on research expeditions collecting samples and data; then I analyze the samples and data back on land. In addition to this, I collaborate with archaeologists in studies of stone tools and secure funding from smaller agencies and contractors to carry out more specific, applied research.

"I also give public lectures on volcanoes, geology, and earth sciences and lead field trips to Kilauea, the active volcano on the island of Hawaii. In addition, I advise museum exhibit staff on technical matters within my area of knowledge, in addition to fielding questions from the public. So, I am very busy day to day and spend about sixty to seventy hours per week on the various aspects of my job. The work atmosphere at the museum and the university are quite pleasant, and I enjoy the interactions I have with my colleagues and students.

"I truly enjoy research because it allows me to pursue questions of my own choosing and to interact with interesting and intelligent people, both colleagues and students. Also, since I don't have to punch a time clock, doing research gives me a lot of time flexibility and a relaxed schedule. The part I enjoy least is the process of research-proposal writing because it takes a considerable amount of time to write a good proposal, and the competition for funds is very keen."

How Kevin T. M. Johnson Got Started

"I was always interested in oceans and volcanoes, and my choice of marine geology seemed natural. Both of my parents introduced me to and encouraged me in science and academic achievement. This probably had the biggest bearing on my career—everything followed from that.

"I earned a B.S. from Penn State, an M.S. from the University of Hawaii, and my Ph.D. from MIT and Woods Hole Oceanographic Institute. Subsequently, I served as a research fellow at the University of Tokyo."

Expert Advice

"I would advise you to be very studious in school and in life in general. Enjoy the world around you and be inquisitive about the natural phenomena you observe every day. Ask questions and think about possible answers."

• • •

INTERVIEW
Glen D. Lawrence, Ph.D.
Professor of Chemistry

Dr. Lawrence has been affiliated with Long Island University since 1985. He received his B.S. in chemistry from Pratt Institute in Brooklyn, New York, his M.A. in chemistry from SUNY at Plattsburgh, New York, and his Ph.D. in biochemistry from Utah State University in Logan, Utah. He served as a science advisor for the U.S. Food and Drug Administration's New York Regional Laboratory from 1988 to 1992, advising analytical chemists in research projects related to drug chemistry.

What the Job Is Really Like

"As a professor of chemistry in a department that offers a master's degree, I am responsible for teaching about nine hours of courses per week during a typical academic year. I teach a wide range of college courses, including any of the following during any given academic year: introductory chemistry for nonscience (liberal arts) majors (three hours of lecture and two hours of lab per week); chemistry for the health sciences (three hours of lecture and two and one-half hours of lab per week); biochemistry to chemistry and molecular biology majors (three hours of lecture and three hours of lab per week); and graduate courses in analytical chemistry, biochemistry, and neurochemistry (each three hours of lecture per week). Occasionally, I offer an elective course for honors students (the one I offered last fall was entitled Drugs in Our Culture). Of course, I don't teach all of these courses in any given year, since it adds up to much more than nine hours per week.

"In addition to teaching, I usually advise undergraduate and graduate students in research projects. This past spring,

I had two undergraduate students working with me on two separate projects. One student was analyzing naltrexone, a morphine-like drug that was being used in a study with hypertensive, stroke-prone rats. The animal study was performed by a colleague in the School of Pharmacy at LIU (Long Island University). Our job in the chemistry department was to measure the drug in blood samples taken from these rats. The amount of blood you can get from a rat is very small (about 0.5 ml), so our procedure had to be suitable for measuring tiny amounts of this potent drug in very small amounts of blood. We were successful in developing the method, after much time was spent trying to fine tune the analytical instrument needed to make these measurements.

"The other project was a study of the effect of combining vitamin C with aspartame (the artificial sweetener known as NutraSweet®) and measuring the products which result from combining these two food additives. We were interested to see if there are any products that could be potentially harmful to human health. Again, this requires the analysis of trace amounts of substances in a complex mixture of things.

"The lab that my students and I work in is very small and cramped (only about seven feet by fifteen feet, including a sink, a hood, a cabinet for glassware, bench space for a pH meter, stirrers for mixing solutions, and some small analytical instruments). Some of the instruments we use are in another large room that contains only special analytical instruments.

"Although the work is not dangerous, we must take the proper precautions when performing some experiments. The materials we work with are usually not explosive in nature, nor are most of them very toxic. However, we must be aware of the things that are toxic or explosive and handle them in a way that is not going to result in a perilous situation.

"Some years ago, I worked as a science advisor for the Food and Drug Administration (FDA). That job required that I go to the FDA labs one day a week and discuss research projects with the analytical chemists there. Their jobs primarily involved analyzing the drugs being sold by pharmaceutical companies. The FDA must use well-established methods for drug analysis, which have undergone extensive testing in both the FDA labs and the pharmaceutical manufacturers' labs. Some of these methods rely on procedures that may be many years old, but newer methods could save much time without sacrificing accuracy. However, any new method must itself be tested before it can become an established method in their protocol. My job was to work with the chemists there to try to streamline the methods used to accomplish efficient and accurate drug analysis.

"One example was a method for analyzing the drugs in nerve gas antidotes for the U.S. Department of Defense. When the Persian Gulf War broke out, nerve gas antidotes had to be removed from storage and tested quickly to make sure they were suitable for use, since much of the stockpile had passed the expiration date. The existing method required approximately forty-five minutes per sample for testing. I tried a different method that I thought would work, and it resulted in decreasing the analysis time to about ten minutes. This isn't a great deal for a few samples, but when there were hundreds of lots of drug samples that had to be analyzed, this decrease in time would mean a savings of weeks or months in analysis time. However, the new method had to be thoroughly tested before it could be implemented. It turned out to be very suitable not only for military samples but for a wide variety of dosage forms, including eye drops and some other medications.

"As a professor, I also serve on various committees around the campus. Though these committees vary from year to year, all take up a substantial amount of time. The committee work may include the evaluation of junior faculty members for promotion and tenure, discussion of new courses and curricula that are being proposed for the university, review of existing courses and programs and the regular re-evaluation of the campus for accreditation, or attention to the day-to-day running of the university.

"In addition, I am often asked to review a master's degree candidate's thesis to determine whether the student meets our approval to obtain a degree. If I am the student's advisor, it may require sitting down with the candidate, advising him or her on how to go about writing a master's thesis, and reading the thesis over many times to make all the necessary corrections before it is submitted to the student's committee. This all occurs after guiding the student through a research project that usually lasts about a year. Although the student doesn't work on the project full time, he or she may put in ten to twenty hours per week doing the research in the lab. This requires developing methods for analyzing certain chemicals that may be of interest to us, collecting a wealth of data to support a hypothesis and analyzing that data to see if it does support the hypothesis, and then finally deciding how to present the data so it will be understandable to others who may be interested.

"Whether in the classroom or the laboratory, teaching can be very exciting. Other times it can be extremely frustrating. Sometimes, students show a genuine interest in the material; other times, I get a whole classroom of students who just don't want to be there (but it is a requirement for them to graduate). Many come into the class dreading it initially but find after a while that we are covering things that can be quite interesting such as the greenhouse effect, global warming, air and water pollution, destruction of the ozone layer, and guidelines about how to keep your body healthy. By the time the students get finished, some of them realize that it was a worthwhile college experience.

"Probably the most rewarding aspect of my job is realized when a student decides to do a special project, either in the form of research in the lab or a library research project, and that student begins to comprehend the complexities of science, especially the life sciences. If I feel that I could instill in another individual the desire to pursue a career in science or just to understand more about how the world works on the molecular level, then I feel I have accomplished my goal. Even if only a handful of my students realize this in my lifetime, I will have passed something on to the next generation."

How Glen D. Lawrence Got Started

"I grew up on a farm in rural New York State and always had a curiosity about how living organisms functioned. However, I had few role models who were scientists in my community (in fact, none that I can think of) and a very poor guidance counselor in high school, so I had little idea what direction I wanted to take after completing high school. I did well in science and math in school and decided to pursue a career in chemistry. As I began studies in chemistry, I realized that my fascination was with biochemistry, so I enrolled in a master's degree program in a chemistry department, with a biochemist as my research advisor. This mentor was recommended by one of my high school friends who had gone to that college as an undergraduate. After completing my master's degree, I had a taste of the academic research life and knew that I wanted to pursue that option. I applied to graduate school in Utah at the suggestion of one of the professors where I had received my M.A. degree and went there to study for the Ph.D. in biochemistry.

"After completing my Ph.D., I applied for a research fellowship to study model systems for photosynthesis, with the support of a NSF (National Science Foundation) Energy-Related Postdoctoral Fellowship. I was always conservation-minded and wanted to do studies on the development of materials that could be used to convert solar energy into useful chemical energy. This specific project was aimed at developing materials that would utilize light to catalyze the splitting of water into hydrogen and oxygen, which could later be used as fuels. After studying this problem for a year in West Germany (1976–77), I came to the realization that it was a difficult task to accomplish (mimicking nature generally is not easy to accomplish in the chemistry laboratory). I spent several years pursuing research at several different laboratories (University of California, Riverside, California, Mt. Sinai, and Columbia University) and found these research opportunities to be extremely valuable to me in broadening my knowledge of science in general and biochemistry, pharmacology, physiology, and toxicology in particular.

"I started at LIU in 1985, while a research fellow in the Institute of Human Nutrition at Columbia University. Funding for my research project was ending and, although I was coauthor of another funded research grant, there had been an administrative error that made me ineligible for financial support from that grant for another year. I therefore actively pursued a teaching position, which was my ultimate career goal. Although I was planning to hold out for a faculty position at a 'research' institution, the master's degree program at LIU, Brooklyn Campus, provided ample opportunity for research, along with interesting possibilities for teaching advanced courses in special areas such as neurochemistry and advanced analytical techniques for biomedical analysis."

Expert Advice

"I was never a specialist, and I don't feel it is necessary to be a specialist to be successful in science, although specialization is the norm. It's important to take advantage of every opportunity to learn, however, whether it is from what seems to be a failure or what seems to be a success. And the most important thing in life is to be satisfied (or happy) with what you are doing. Some people feel it is necessary to work at a job to make money, so you can enjoy yourself in the relatively few hours you may have to yourself. But if you enjoy your work, you will not have to spend so much of your money trying to get away from your work."

● ● ●

INTERVIEW
Charles L. Dumoulin, Ph.D.
Research Scientist

Dr. Dumoulin serves as a physicist in the field of medicine. He has been on staff at General Electric's Research and Development Center in Schenectady, New York, since 1984. In 1996, he received the Center's highest honor, its Coolidge Fellowship Award, which recognizes sustained contribution to science or engineering. Dr. Dumoulin was honored for his pioneering contributions to magnetic resonance imaging (MRI). He has published eighty-three peer-reviewed papers, twenty-four chapters in books, sixty-one issued patents, and he has eleven patents pending.

What the Job Is Really Like

"For the last thirteen years, I have been working as a physicist in the field of medicine. I have worked primarily to develop new ways to perform diagnostic and interventional procedures with Magnetic Resonance Imaging (MRI) scanners. Major projects which I have led, or been a part of, include: MR spectroscopy, MR angiography (use of radio frequency signals to follow devices in real-time), MR measurements of kidney function, MR tracking of interventional devices in real-time, cardiac MR imaging, and use of MR to increase basic understanding of flow physiology in blood vessels.

"Although I'm paid to work forty hours per week, I typically work eight to nine hours per day and frequently a few hours during the weekend. Even when I'm not working, I often find myself thinking about problems from work. Some of my most productive moments occur while trying to fall asleep and driving to or from work.

"As a scientist working in industry, my job is somewhat different than that of an academic scientist working in a university. For example, I have to justify my work as having some relevance to my company. Consequently, most of what I do can be called applied science rather than basic science.

"The work atmosphere here is relatively relaxed, yet there is always a certain intensity of purpose. I am surrounded by extremely capable colleagues who have been trained in a number of different scientific disciplines (computer science, physical chemistry, physics, astrophysics, medicine, electrical engineering). We tend to work in ad hoc teams, and conflicts are rare. Every Friday we meet to discuss topics as diverse as life in the universe, politics, or even Dilbert.

"A nice aspect of my job is that every day brings unique challenges and tasks. A typical day begins with the reading and answering of E-mail. I interact with many people in Europe and Japan, and we have found that E-mail is the best way to communicate. One or two days each week, I sign up to use the MRI scanner in our building. I spend those days testing new ideas and performing experiments. When I'm not in the lab, I can usually be found at my desk writing (E-mail, memos, papers, etc.) or in meetings with my colleagues.

"My job frequently requires me to travel. My trips often take me to conferences where I speak about my work and listen to other scientists speak about theirs. I find that these talks are often a great source of inspiration. Other trips take me to different research hospitals around the world where I work with doctors to develop and evaluate new ways of using MRI scanners.

"To me, the best part of this career is the intellectual challenge of finding creative solutions to problems, the exposure to new ideas within and beyond my profession, and working on medical diagnostic methods that have direct relevance to patients. I also enjoy the latitude I have to define my own research agenda (although I wish I had more), working with some of the best scientists and engineers in the world, and the opportunity to talk to students of all ages about science and technology.

"The more negative aspects of this career include the fact that things get in the way of productivity, and it is difficult to secure funding for projects and patent protection for all of my inventions. Also, there is a lack of tenure in the industry, compensation for scientists is not commensurate with their contributions to society, and there is a lack of wide-ranging opportunities for people in my specialty."

How Charles L. Dumoulin Got Started

"Although I was always fascinated by science as a child (and high school showed me I had a knack for science and math), my original career plan was to become a military officer. When I learned that my eyesight was too poor, I changed my plans and went to Florida State University, choosing chemistry as my major. After school and during summer vacations, I worked in a television and appliance repair shop and realized that I enjoyed learning how things work (televisions, radios, washing machines, refrigerators, etc.). I also learned that the best way to understand something was to take it apart, fix it, and put it back together. I found solving problems to be most enjoyable. As I became a researcher, I found that the most fun problems to tackle were those which required creative solutions and addressed real-life problems. I also found that, unlike many fields, science generally dealt with questions that have objective and provable answers.

"Subsequently, I earned a Ph.D. from Florida State University in analytical chemistry in 1981. After I received my Ph.D., I moved with my thesis professor to Syracuse University where I became a nontenure-track assistant professor. For three years, I helped run a lab, did some research, and was cofounder of a small company. I came to realize, however, that this environment was not allowing me to develop as a researcher.

"I then moved to GE's Research and Development Center where I changed my focus from Nuclear Magnetic Resonance Spectroscopy for chemistry to the related topic of Magnetic Resonance (MR) for medical applications."

Expert Advice

"I'd recommend to all prospective scientists that you remain as broad as possible. Scientific success often occurs by the synergistic combination of two or more existing ideas from different disciplines.

"It's important to stay focused on competing projects. But somehow you must concentrate on each project at every stage of its being. And usually a project is not considered complete until a publication (memo, paper, patent application, etc.) is submitted.

"It is always in your best interests to use the golden rule when dealing with everyone. Be particularly sensitive to the issue of sharing credit with your coworkers. Virtually all discoveries are accomplished as a result of the efforts of many—be sure everyone gets their just portion of the rewards!"

● ● ●

INTERVIEW
Eric S. Posmentier, Ph.D.
Professor of Physics and Mathematics

Dr. Posmentier serves as Professor of Physics and Mathematics at the Brooklyn Campus of Long Island University, Brooklyn, New York. He earned a B.S. from the City College of New York (in physics) in 1964 and a Ph.D. from Columbia University in 1968 (in geophysics). At a time when global warming was still viewed with skepticism by many scientists, Posmentier and his colleagues at Columbia University, using data from the tropical Pacific Ocean, published evidence that global warming had begun. In addition, Posmentier is working with scientists at the Harvard/Smithsonian Astrophysical Observatory to study variations of the brightness of the sun.

What the Job Is Really Like

"On most days, I am in my office for up to eleven hours. I spend roughly half my time preparing classes, lecturing, meeting with students, writing, grading exams, and meeting with other professors to discuss academic matters. The other half of my time is spent reading and doing my own research. Occasionally, my research has taken me to mountains to observe air, clouds, rocks, and forests, or by boat or scuba to rivers, lakes, bays, and the ocean to observe the water and its movement. Most of my research time, however, is spent at my desk or computer. I tend to be involved in several things at once, so my typical day is busy and hectic, but there are always times when I can change the pace by having informal discussions with colleagues about my work or theirs. The ideas that come out of these informal discussions are frequently as important, in their own way, as the results of the long, disciplined hours spent alone writing, deriving mathematics, or computing. When I am deeply engrossed in a research problem, it often 'comes home' with me, and I find myself working on it in the evenings and weekends, as well.

"The best part of the work is the moment a new concept is discovered and the moment when my students catch on to a concept I am teaching. Least favorite is grading, grading, grading."

How Eric S. Posmentier Got Started

"Ever since elementary school, I have been fascinated by nature and curious about explanations of natural phenomena. I was drawn to any kind of scientific activity I had the opportunity to pursue such as collecting rocks, dissecting a dead bird, or experimenting with a chemistry set inherited from an older cousin. By high school, I knew that I wanted a career in the physical sciences or mathematics. In college, I discovered that geophysical sciences (physics of the atmosphere, oceans, and solid earth) held the greatest attraction for me. That is what I have concentrated on ever since, until I recently added quantum mechanics to my active research.

"The development of my interests is largely the gift of teachers and professors who gave me confidence in myself and who shared their excitement of discovering knowledge, skills, and concepts. Two particularly formative experiences stand out in my memory. One was a Bronx High School of Science sophomore course devoted to individual biology research projects. In that course, I learned how challenging it is to design an original experiment, and how rewarding it is to succeed. The other experience was the opportunity to work part time (while still in college) with graduate students and Ph.D.s, in a research laboratory at Columbia University. There, I discovered how satisfying it can be to apply to unsolved problems the concepts and skills I was still in the process of acquiring in my classes, make some progress, and uncover still new questions.

"While in college, I recognized that geophysics combined several of my greatest passions: studying the exciting frontiers of understanding our planet, applying the fascinating disciplines of physics and mathematics, and spending time in the outdoors observing. I am especially attracted to problems which cross specializations within which many scientists confine themselves; for example, the physics of global warming and the economics of energy use, or ocean currents and the fishing industry, or seismic detection of earthquakes and explosions and the politics of disarmament. As a professor, I also enjoy transmitting my knowledge of and excitement for science to the next generation."

Expert Advice

"I would advise that you emphasize the fundamental sciences and mathematics in your courses. You should study interdisciplinary applications such as environmental science or marine science only in addition to—never instead of—physics, chemistry, biology, and mathematics. The latter are the foundation upon which all the rest will have to stand. Find a teacher or professor who is willing to guide you in formulating and working on an individual research problem for a week, a year, or a lifetime."

●   ●   ●

FOR MORE INFORMATION

General information on career opportunities and earnings for chemists is available from:

> American Chemical Society, Department of Career Services, 1155 16th St. N.W., Washington, D.C. 20036

Information on federal job opportunities is available from local offices of state employment services or offices of the United States Office of Personnel Management, located in major metropolitan areas.

Sources of Additional Information for Physicists and Astronomers

General information on career opportunities in physics is available from:

> American Institute of Physics, Career Planning and Placement, One Physics Ellipse, College Park, MD 20740-3843

> American Physical Society, Education Department, One Physics Ellipse, College Park, MD 20740-3844

For a pamphlet containing information on careers in astronomy, send your request to:

> American Astronomical Society, Education Office, University of Texas, Department of Astronomy, Austin, TX 78712-1083

Information on training and career opportunities for geologists is available from:

> American Geological Institute, 4220 King St., Alexandria, VA 22302-1507

> Geological Society of America, P.O. Box 9140, 3300 Penrose Pl., Boulder, CO 80301

> American Association of Petroleum Geologists, Communications Department, P.O. Box 979, Tulsa, OK 74101

Information on training and career opportunities for geophysicists is available from:

American Geophysical Union, 2000 Florida Ave. N.W., Washington, D.C. 20009

A list of curricula in colleges and universities offering programs in oceanography and related fields is available from:

Marine Technology Society, 1828 L St. N.W., Suite 906, Washington, D.C. 20036

Information on federal job opportunities is available from local offices of state employment services or branches of the United States Office of Personnel Management, located in major metropolitan areas.

Information on career opportunities in meteorology is available from:

American Meteorological Society, 45 Beacon St., Boston, MA 02108

National Oceanic and Atmospheric Administration, Human Resources Management Office, 1315 East West Hwy., Route Code OA/22, Silver Spring, MD 20910

CHAPTER 4 Careers in Engineering

🎓 **EDUCATION**
B.A./B.S. required; postgraduate
work recommended

$$$ **SALARY**
$30,000 to $60,000

OVERVIEW
Engineers

Engineers apply the theories and principles of science and mathematics to the economical solution of practical technical problems. Usually, their work is the link between a scientific discovery and its commercial application. Engineers design machinery, products, systems, and processes for efficient and economical performance. They design industrial machinery and equipment for manufacturing defense-related goods and weapons systems for the armed forces. They design, plan, and supervise the construction of buildings, highways, and rapid transit systems. They also design and develop systems for control and automation of manufacturing, business, and management processes.

Engineers consider many factors in developing a new product. For example, in developing an industrial robot, they determine precisely what function it needs to perform, design and test the necessary components, fit them together in an integrated plan, and evaluate the design's overall effectiveness, cost, reliability, and safety. This process applies to products as different as chemicals, computers, gas turbines, helicopters, and toys.

In addition to design and development, many engineers work in testing, production, or maintenance. They supervise production in factories, determine the causes of breakdowns, and test manufactured products to maintain quality. They also estimate the time and cost to complete projects. Some engineers work in management or in sales, where an engineering background enables them to discuss the technical aspects of a product and assist in planning its installation or use.

Engineers often use computers to simulate and test how a machine, structure, or system operates. Many engineers also use computer-aided design systems to produce and analyze designs. They spend a great deal of time writing reports and consulting with other engineers, as complex projects often require an interdisciplinary team of engineers. Supervisory engineers are responsible for major components or entire projects.

Most engineers specialize. More than twenty-five major engineering specialties are recognized by professional societies, and within the major branches are numerous subdivisions. Structural, environmental, and transportation engineering, for example, are subdivisions of civil engineering. Engineers also may specialize in one industry such as motor vehicles, or in one field of technology such as propulsion or guidance systems.

Descriptions of ten separate engineering branches follow:

AEROSPACE ENGINEERS Aerospace engineers design, develop, test, and help manufacture commercial and military aircraft, missiles, and spacecraft. They develop new technologies for use in commercial aviation, defense systems, and space exploration, often specializing in areas like structural design, guidance, navigation and control, instrumentation and communication, or production methods. They also may specialize in a particular type of aerospace product such as commercial transports, helicopters, spacecraft, or rockets. Aerospace engineers may be experts in aerodynamics, propulsion, thermodynamics, structures, celestial mechanics, acoustics, or guidance and control systems.

CHEMICAL ENGINEERS Chemical engineers apply the principles of chemistry and engineering to solve problems involving the production or use of chemicals. Most work in the production of chemicals and chemical products. They design equipment and develop processes for manufacturing chemicals, plan and test methods of manufacturing the products, and supervise production. Chemical engineers also work in industries other than chemical manufacturing such as electronics or aircraft manufacturing. Because the knowledge and duties of chemical engineers cut across many fields, they apply principles of chemistry, physics, mathematics, and mechanical and electrical engineering in their work. They frequently specialize in a particular operation such as oxidation or polymerization. Others specialize in a particular area such as pollution control or the production of a specific product like automotive plastics or chlorine bleach.

CIVIL ENGINEERS Civil engineers work in the oldest branch of engineering. They design and supervise the construction of roads, airports, tunnels, bridges, water supply and sewage systems, and buildings. Major specialties within civil engineering are structural, water resources, environmental, construction, transportation, and geotechnical engineering.

Many civil engineers hold supervisory or administrative positions, ranging from supervisor of a construction site to city engineer. Others may work in design, construction, research, and teaching.

ELECTRICAL AND ELECTRONICS ENGINEERS Electrical and electronics engineers design, develop, test, and supervise the manufacture of electrical and electronic equipment. Electrical equipment includes power-generating and transmission equipment used by electric utilities, as well as electric motors, machinery controls, and lighting and wiring in buildings, automobiles, and aircraft. Electronic equipment includes radar, computer hardware, and communications and video equipment.

The specialties of electrical and electronics engineers include several major areas such as power generation, transmission, and distribution; communications; computer electronics; and electrical equipment manufacturing; or they may include a subdivision of these areas such as industrial robot control systems or aviation electronics. Electrical and electronics engineers design new products, write performance requirements, and develop maintenance schedules. They also test equipment, solve operating problems, and estimate the time and cost of engineering projects.

INDUSTRIAL ENGINEERS Industrial engineers determine the most effective ways for an organization to use the basic factors of production: people, machines, materials, information, and energy to make or process a product. Industrial engineers are the bridge between management and operations. They are more concerned with increasing productivity through the management of people, methods of business organization, and technology than are engineers in other specialties, who generally work more with products or processes.

To solve organizational, production, and related problems most efficiently, industrial engineers carefully study the product and its requirements, design manufacturing and information systems, and use mathematical analysis methods such as operations research to meet those requirements. They develop management control systems to aid in financial planning and cost analysis, design production planning and control systems to coordinate activities and control product quality, and design or improve systems for the physical distribution of goods and services. Industrial engineers conduct surveys to find plant locations with the best combination of raw materials, transportation, and costs. They also develop wage and salary administration systems and job evaluation programs. Many industrial engineers move into management positions because the work is closely related.

MECHANICAL ENGINEERS Mechanical engineers plan and design tools, engines, machines, and other mechanical equipment. They design and develop power-producing machines such as internal combustion engines, steam and gas turbines, and jet and rocket engines. They also design and develop power-using machines such as refrigeration and air-conditioning equipment, robots, machine tools, materials handling systems, and industrial production equipment.

The work of mechanical engineers varies by industry and function. Specialties include, among others, applied mechanics, design engineering, heat transfer, power plant engineering, pressure vessels and piping, and underwater technology. Mechanical engineers design tools needed by other engineers for their work.

Mechanical engineering is the broadest engineering discipline, extending across many interdependent specialties. Mechanical engineers may work in production operations, maintenance, or technical sales. Many are administrators or managers.

METALLURGICAL, CERAMIC, AND MATERIALS ENGINEERS Metallurgical, ceramic, and materials engineers develop new types of metal alloys, ceramics, composites, and other materials that meet special requirements. Examples are graphite golf club shafts that are light but stiff, ceramic tiles on the space shuttle that protect it from burning up during reentry, and the alloy turbine blades in a jet engine.

Most metallurgical engineers work in one of the three main branches of metallurgy—extractive or chemical, physical, and mechanical or process. Extractive metallurgists are concerned with removing metals from ores and refining and alloying them to obtain useful metal. Physical metallurgists study the nature, structure, and physical properties of metals and their alloys and methods of processing them into final products. Mechanical metallurgists develop and improve metalworking processes such as casting, forging, rolling, and drawing.

Ceramic engineers develop new ceramic materials and methods for making ceramic materials into useful products. Ceramics include all nonmetallic, inorganic materials that require high temperatures in their processing. Ceramic engineers work on products as diverse as glassware, semiconductors, automobile and aircraft engine components, fiber-optic telephone lines, tile, and electric power line insulators.

Materials engineers evaluate technical requirements and material specifications to develop materials that can be used, for example, to reduce the weight but not the strength of an object. Materials engineers also test and evaluate materials and develop new materials such as the composite materials now being used in "stealth" aircraft.

A materials engineer uses X-ray photoelectron spectroscopy to examine the structure of a new ceramic.

MINING ENGINEERS Mining engineers find, extract, and prepare metals and minerals for use by manufacturing industries. They design open-pit and underground mines, supervise the construction of mine shafts and tunnels in underground operations, and devise methods for transporting minerals to processing plants. Mining engineers are responsible for the safe, economical, and environmentally sound operation of mines. Some mining engineers work with geologists and metallurgical engineers to locate and appraise new ore deposits. Others develop new mining equipment or direct mineral processing operations to separate minerals from the dirt, rock, and other materials with which they are mixed. Mining engineers frequently specialize in the mining of one mineral or metal such as coal or gold.

With increased emphasis on protecting the environment, many mining engineers work solving problems related to land reclamation and water and air pollution.

A mining engineer examines the plans of the current mine and the next phase to determine the best location for a conveyor system.

NUCLEAR ENGINEERS Nuclear engineers conduct research on nuclear energy and radiation. They design, develop, monitor, and operate nuclear power plants used to generate electricity and power navy ships. They may work on the nuclear fuel cycle; fusion energy; the production, handling, and use of nuclear fuel; and the safe disposal of waste produced by nuclear energy. Some specialize in the development of nuclear weapons; others develop industrial and medical uses for radioactive materials such as equipment to diagnose and treat medical problems.

PETROLEUM ENGINEERS Petroleum engineers explore for workable reservoirs containing oil or natural gas. When one is discovered, petroleum engineers work to achieve the maximum profitable recovery from the reservoir by determining and developing the most efficient production methods.

Because only a small proportion of the oil and gas in a reservoir will flow out under natural forces, petroleum engineers develop and use various enhanced recovery methods. These include injecting water, chemicals, or steam into an oil reservoir to force more of the oil out, and horizontal drilling or fracturing to connect more of a gas reservoir to a well. Since even the best methods in use today recover only a portion of the oil and gas in a reservoir, petroleum engineers work to find ways to increase this proportion.

Branches of engineering not covered in detail here but in which there are established college programs include the following: architectural engineering (the design of a building's internal support structure), biomedical engineering (the application of engineering to medical and physiological problems), environmental engineering (a growing discipline involved with identifying, solving, and alleviating environmental problems), and marine engineering (the design and installation of ship machinery and propulsion systems).

Engineers in each branch have knowledge and training that can be applied to many fields. Electrical and electronics engineers, for example, work in the medical, computer, missile guidance, and power distribution fields. Because there are many separate problems to solve in a large engineering project, engineers in one field often work closely with specialists in other scientific, engineering, and business occupations.

TRAINING

A bachelor's degree in engineering from an accredited engineering program is usually required for beginning engineering jobs. College graduates with a degree in mathematics or a physical science may occasionally qualify for some engineering jobs, especially in engineering specialties in high demand. Most engineering degrees are granted in branches such as electrical, mechanical, or civil engineering. However, engineers trained in one branch may work in another. This flexibility allows employers to meet staffing needs in new technologies and specialties where engineers are in short supply. It also allows engineers to shift to fields with better employment prospects or to ones that match their interests more closely.

In addition to offering the standard engineering degree, many colleges and universities offer degrees in engineering technology, which are offered as either two- or four-year sequences. These programs prepare students for practical design and production work rather than for jobs that require more theoretical, scientific, and mathematical knowledge. Graduates of four-year technology programs may get jobs similar to those obtained by graduates with a bachelor's degree in engineering. Some employers regard them as having skills between those of a technician and an engineer.

Graduate training is essential for engineering faculty positions but is not required for the majority of entry-level engineering jobs. Many engineers obtain graduate degrees in engineering or business administration to learn new technology, broaden their education, and enhance promotion opportunities; others obtain law degrees and become attorneys. Many high-level executives in government and industry began their careers as engineers.

About 340 colleges and universities offer a bachelor's degree in engineering, and nearly 300 offer a bachelor's degree in engineering technology, although not all are accredited programs. Although most institutions offer programs in the larger branches of engineering, only a few offer some of the smaller specialties. Also, programs of the same title may vary in content. For example, some programs emphasize industrial practices, preparing students for a job in industry, while others are more theoretical and are therefore better for students preparing to take graduate work. Students should investigate curricula and check accreditations carefully before selecting a college. Admissions requirements for undergraduate engineering schools include courses in advanced high school mathematics and the physical sciences.

Bachelor's degree programs in engineering are typically designed to last four years, but many students find that it takes between four and five years to complete their studies. In a typical four-year college curriculum, the first two years are spent studying basic sciences (mathematics, physics, and chemistry), introductory engineering, as well as the humanities, social sciences, and English. In the last two years, most courses are in engineering, usually with a concentration in one branch. For example, the last two years of an aerospace program might include courses such as fluid mechanics, heat transfer, applied aerodynamics, analytical mechanics, flight vehicle design, trajectory dynamics, and aerospace propulsion systems. Some programs offer a general engineering curriculum; students then specialize in graduate school or on the job.

A few engineering schools and two-year colleges have agreements whereby the two-year college provides the initial engineering education and the engineering school automatically admits students for their last two years. In addition, a few engineering schools have arrangements whereby a student spends three years in a liberal arts college studying pre-engineering subjects and two years in the engineering school and receives a bachelor's degree from each. Some colleges and universities offer five-year master's degree programs.

Some five- or even six-year cooperative plans combine classroom study and practical work, permitting students to gain valuable experience and finance part of their education.

All fifty U.S. states and the District of Columbia require registration for engineers whose work may affect life, health, or property, or who offer their services to the public. In 1994, between 250,000 and 300,000 engineers were registered. Registration generally requires a degree from an engineering program accredited by the Accreditation Board for Engineering and Technology, four years of relevant work experience, and successful completion of a state examination. Some states will not register people with degrees in engineering technology. Engineers may be registered in several states.

Beginning engineering graduates usually do routine work under the supervision of experienced engineers and, in larger companies, may also receive formal classroom or seminar-type training. As they gain knowledge and experience, they are assigned more difficult tasks with greater independence to develop designs, solve problems, and make decisions. Engineers may become technical specialists or may supervise a staff or team of engineers and technicians. Some eventually become engineering managers or enter other managerial, management support, or sales jobs.

Engineers should be able to work as part of a team and should be creative, analytical, and detail-oriented. In addition, engineers should be able to communicate well, both orally and in writing.

JOB OUTLOOK

Employment opportunities in engineering are expected to be good through the year 2005 because employment is expected to increase about as fast as the average for all occupations, while the number of degrees granted in engineering is expected to remain near present levels through the year 2005.

Many of the jobs in engineering are related to national defense. Because defense expenditures have declined, employment growth and job outlook for engineers may not be as strong as in times when defense expenditures were increasing. However, graduating engineers will continue to be in demand for jobs in engineering and other areas, possibly even at the same time other engineers, especially defense industry engineers, are being laid off.

Employers will rely on engineers to further increase productivity as they increase investment in plants and equipment to expand output of goods and services. In addition, competitive pressures and advancing technology will force companies to improve and update product designs more frequently. Finally, more engineers will be needed to improve deteriorating roads, bridges, water and pollution control systems, and other public facilities.

Freshman engineering enrollments began declining in 1983, and the number of bachelor's degrees in engineering began declining in 1987. Although it is difficult to project engineering enrollments, this decline may continue through the late 1990s because the total college-age population is projected to decline. Furthermore, the proportion of students interested in engineering careers has declined as prospects for college graduates in other fields have improved and interest in other programs has increased. Also, engineering schools have restricted enrollments, especially in defense-related fields such as aerospace engineering, to match the reduced opportunities in defense-related industries.

Only a relatively small proportion of engineers leave the profession each year. Despite this, over 70 percent of all job openings will arise from replacement needs. A greater proportion of replacement openings is created by engineers who transfer to management, sales, or other professional specialty occupations than by those who leave the labor force.

Most industries are less likely to lay off engineers than other workers. Many engineers work on long-term research and development projects or in other activities that may continue even during recessions. In industries such as electronics and aerospace, however, large government cutbacks in defense or research and development have resulted in significant layoffs for engineers.

New computer-aided design systems have improved the design process, enabling engineers to produce or modify designs much more rapidly. Engineers now produce and analyze many more design variations before selecting a final one. However, this technology is not expected to limit employment opportunities.

It is important for engineers to continue their education throughout their careers because much of their value to their employer depends on their knowledge of the latest technology. The pace of technological change varies by engineering specialty and industry. Engineers in high-technology areas such as advanced electronics may find that technical knowledge can become obsolete rapidly. Even those who continue their education are vulnerable if the particular technology or product they have specialized in becomes obsolete. Engineers who have not kept current in their field may find themselves passed over for promotions and are vulnerable should layoffs occur. On the other hand, it is often these high-technology areas that offer the greatest challenges, the most interesting work, and the highest salaries. Therefore, the choice of engineering specialty and employer involves an assessment of both the potential rewards and the risk of technological obsolescence.

SALARIES

Starting salaries for engineers with a bachelor's degree are significantly higher than starting salaries of bachelor's degree graduates in other fields. According to the National Association of Colleges and Employers, engineering graduates with a bachelor's degree averaged about $34,100 a year in private industry in 1994; those with a master's degree and no experience averaged $40,200 a year; and those with a Ph.D. averaged $55,300. Starting salaries for those with the bachelor's degree vary by branch:

Aerospace	$30,860
Chemical	39,204
Civil	29,809
Electrical	34,840
Industrial	33,267
Mechanical	35,051
Metallurgical	33,429
Mining	32,638
Nuclear	33,603
Petroleum	38,286

The average annual salary for engineers in the federal government in nonsupervisory, supervisory, and managerial positions was $58,080 in 1995.

RELATED FIELDS

Engineers apply the principles of physical science and mathematics in their work. Other workers who use scientific and mathematical principles include physical scientists, life scientists, computer scientists, mathematicians, engineering and science technicians, and architects.

INTERVIEW
Mary Shafer, M.S.
Senior Aerospace Engineer

Mary Shafer is a senior aerospace engineer for NASA at the Dryden Flight Research Center. The Dryden Flight Research Center is considered NASA's premier installation for aeronautical flight research. Located at Edwards Air Force Base in California on the Mojave Desert, the center celebrated its fiftieth anniversary in 1996. Dryden has grown from an initial group of five engineers in 1946 to a facility with more than 460 NASA government employees and about the same number of civilian contractor personnel. In addition to carrying out aeronautical research, the center also supports the space shuttle program as a primary and backup landing site and as a facility to test and validate design concepts and systems used in development and operation.

What the Job Is Really Like

"My projects vary, but right now, in addition to a number of small flying-qualities research projects, I'm working on one particular experiment called the aerospy. It is my responsibility to look at an airplane's various flying qualities to make sure that any modifications that are made are safe. We must fulfill our priority of being able to fly airplanes that are structurally sound.

"Most of my day is spent either talking with pilots, studying data on various computers, visiting the simulation area to see how the plane is flying, watching the input of our new ideas, or observing what the airplane looks like with the new lift, drag, or whatever the case may be. Then we put the results of our efforts in the simulator, so that the pilots can fly the planes and determine if the 'real' planes will fly as we want them to. For example, we focus on issues like: Are we going to have enough runway to take off? Are we going to have enough thrust? Will it go forward instead of falling out of the sky?

"My other real interest lies in how the aircraft pilot system works and what the pilot needs to get from the airplane in order to feel that it's a good airplane or a bad airplane. In his opening sentence in *Anna Karenina*, Tolstoy says 'All happy families are alike, but each unhappy family is unhappy in its own way.' Well, the same is true of airplanes; a good airplane is not very interesting to a quality engineer, but a bad airplane is fascinating.

"I work fairly regular hours. However, it's my understanding that this is somewhat less common in the university setting. The situation here is that we'll occasionally have a surge of work. For instance, I've got to write a paper which is due in three months, so I'll probably do that on weekends but then go back to a normal work schedule."

How Mary Shafer Got Started

"As a high school senior in the early sixties, I attended a National Science Foundation course at UCLA between my junior and senior years. The subject happened to be meteorology, but it gave me a chance to see that science and research provided a way to explain the world around me, which I felt was interesting and important. Then I got a summer job working for the U.S. Air Force, where I discovered I liked being near airplanes. I began my college career at UCLA as a chemistry major but later switched to engineering. I spent subsequent summers working for NASA, and I decided I truly wanted to focus my career on airplanes and flight research. And I was very lucky. I had a lot of good people to work with, a number of individuals who were willing to explain things to me and provide me with examples in everyday life that related to aerodynamics and fluid mechanics.

"During the summers at NASA, I began by reducing data, working with a ruler in engineering units, plotting the information on graph paper with orange carbon behind it. I wrote a couple of smaller programs which impressed everybody (because at that point few people could do that). The next year, I progressed to writing computer matrix manipulations designed to measure trial-time-stability analysis during flight. That was really interesting because it was at that point that I started to understand the rules that governed how airplanes flew.

"I earned my bachelor's degree and came back and worked another summer writing quality programs for some of the engineers. Then I went back and got my master's degree. The next summer, I was writing with engineers and even married one.

"I began working as a computer programmer writing follow-up programs for the X-24B and then worked for Lockheed on the FA certification of the L-1011. I moved on to McDonnell Douglas and McDonnell Douglas Aircraft and then worked on the F-4 airplane and the initial acceptance testing of the F-15. Then I accepted a position in the air force as a systems designer working on writing programs. Finally, I came back over to NASA and got a job as a controls engineer.

"NASA employs aeronautical engineers, mechanical engineers, electrical engineers, meteorologists, and physicists. We cover a broad range of disciplines: engineering and the hard sciences, chemistry, physics, meteorology, and math. It's important that you know math and extremely important that you know how to program and use the computer. Also, you need to know how to write clearly with grammatical accuracy. There's no point in doing research if you can't write it down clearly and well enough that people can understand what you did, how you did it, why you did it, and what happened when you did it. Flexibility is another important quality for researchers because you don't know how your attempts are going to come out, and you have to be able to build upon your successes or shift gears when the outcome isn't as you planned. People who are unable to deal with uncertainty may find that research is not a good field for them. And, in this line of work, a robust ego is a nice thing to have."

Expert Advice

"Research is essentially a mutual endeavor. When you begin a project, you never really know what will be gained from your efforts, what will be gleaned, or how the new information might be used. It is only in the later stages of your work that you may be able to ascertain exactly how the information gained from your research will affect others on a grander scale. This is what provides fulfillment for all scientists and engineers—uncovering or discovering information that can benefit the world in which we live."

●　　●　　●

INTERVIEW
Lieutenant Commander Joseph W. McVeigh, M.S.
Chief of Operations

Lieutenant Commander Joseph W. McVeigh is Chief of the Operations Division of the U.S. Army's Air Worthiness Qualification Test Directorate.

What the Job Is Really Like

"The army has a small group of officers (approximately 2,000) from the ranks of captain to colonel that make up the Acquisition Corps. These officers come from all branches of the army (infantry, aviation, field artillery, and so forth). The purpose of the Acquisition Corps is to have an elite group of officers that procure all of the equipment, weapons, and vehicles that the army requires for its operations. This includes research and development, test and evaluation, program management, and staff/support functions.

"For clarification, the army differentiates between research and development (R & D) and test and evaluation (T & E). I'm not sure if they are considered one and the same in the civilian world. The research and development personnel work in the army laboratories and at universities doing basic research and concept exploration. I work in the T & E area. We do the developmental testing of hardware (testing to specifications) and operational testing (testing with troops to determine operational stability—Does it work the way it's supposed to?).

"Currently, I'm stationed at Edwards Air Force Base with U.S. Army Airworthiness Qualification Test Directorate, where they conduct airworthiness flight testing of army helicopters and airplanes. When I first arrived, I performed as a flight test engineer on several tests, including work on the OH-58D helicopter and the MH-47E helicopter.

"As a flight test engineer, I was in charge of the flights. I told the experimental test pilot what profile to fly, how to fly it, and for how long. Designing the test plan was one of my major responsibilities. It was the road map that everyone would follow to conduct the test. I also coordinated the flight crews and crash rescue crews, test budgets, and personnel overtime.

"On a typical day as a flight test engineer, I would come in at 7:00 A.M. and pick up where I had left off on reducing data from the previous day's (or week's) flights. If a test flight was scheduled for that day for my aircraft, I briefed the crews, maintenance personnel, safety and crash rescue, and flight operations personnel on what we were doing and the schedule for the day. I would then coordinate the aircraft's preparation for the flight (if it wasn't done the previous afternoon). My responsibilities also included preparing the flight data card, operating all the test equipment and data recording equipment on board, and cueing the pilots as what to do next during the flight.

"If I didn't have a flight going that day but someone else did, I would fly a chase aircraft alongside them as they flew their profile (for safety). The chase pilot coordinates the airspace and makes all the radio calls to ground and air traffic control and range control.

"I remained in that job for one year and then was selected for my current position as chief of the operations division. I and the people under me are in charge of the organization's budget, flight operations, photography and graphic arts support, technical publications support, and business office. In addition, I fly in support of flight tests here and at other remote sites that we have jurisdiction over."

How Joseph W. McVeigh Got Started

"I've always wanted to fly, and I decided the best way to do this was to join one of the armed services. I went to the University of Montana in Missoula because it was convenient and inexpensive (and my parents lived there). Air force and army ROTC were located there and were always ready to welcome a new cadet. I joined army ROTC during my sophomore year, completed school, and received a B.S. degree in forestry in 1979. (I subsequently received an M.S. degree in computer resource management from Webster University in St. Louis, Missouri.) Once I graduated and got commissioned as a second lieutenant, I was off to Fort Knox, Kentucky, for the Armor Officers Basic Course. During the Basic Course, I applied for flight school and was accepted. While I was at my first flying assignment following flight school, I was selected to support an aviation test for a new type of radio. The test lasted three months, and, after it was over, I realized this is what I wanted to do in the army. Although the test organization I was supporting (the Aviation Board, Ft. Rucker, Alabama) was small (thirty officers), I was lucky enough to get assigned there.

"My previous jobs (T & E- and R & D-related) include test project officer, where I conducted operational tests on several aircraft-related components, and UH-60 plans officer, where

I initiated test plans for operational testing for future programs. Both of these jobs were done while I was at Ft. Rucker as a captain. When I moved to the aviations systems command in St. Louis, I performed for one year as an aeronautical engineer working on the design of various cockpits to provide human factors input on design, layout, safety-of-flight crucial items, etc. My second job (for one and a half years) in St. Louis was doing administrative-type work for two general officers. My third job (for two years) was coordinating joint programs with the navy and air force so that we all worked toward using the same equipment in the future. I also worked with Canada, England, and Saudi Arabia to initiate joint laboratory-type work between these countries and the U.S. Army."

Expert Advice

"This type of career is designed for a particular type of person—one who is dedicated to his or her work and who sees things in a larger perspective, one who wants to provide the world with something better than what we already have."

● ● ●

INTERVIEW
Ernestine Meyers, M.S.
Senior Environmental Engineer

Ernestine Meyers serves as Senior Environmental Engineer for the Division of Sanitation Facilities Construction in the Office of Environmental Health and Engineering Office of the United States Public Health Service in Albuquerque, New Mexico.

What the Job Is Really Like

"A typical day consists of working on the plans and designs for a pueblo spring house, spending time with the surveyors who are doing the groundwork for some of my projects, working on specifications or proposals for future projects, dealing with contractors, or helping out the other engineers when they have any technical questions.

"My next goal is to obtain my professional registration. For this, I need to take an eight-hour exam which covers all areas of engineering. I'm sure this will not be my most pleasant experience, but it will lead to my promotion to District Engineer, and that's what's important."

How Ernestine Meyers Got Started

"While I was growing up, my summers were spent out in the field with my father. That's how I became familiar with inner workings of the Indian Health Service. He worked for the agency as an environmental health technician for thirty-two years. Together, we would travel to different reservations, where I would observe what he did. I met and talked with engineers and got to know what they were responsible for. And, of course, I helped whenever I could. With my father as a role model and a love for science and the outdoors, I found my career direction. Today, I hold the position of Senior Environmental Engineer for the Division of Sanitation Facilities Construction in the Office of Environmental Health and Engineering Office of the U.S. Public Health Service in Albuquerque, New Mexico.

"Born on a New Mexican pueblo reservation, I am the oldest of four children. Given my choice to attend the Bureau of Indian Affairs (BIA) or a public school in a nearby town, I decided to attend public school a few miles from the pueblo. Each day, I traveled to school on a bus driven by my grandfather. Some of my friends went to BIA schools, and some went to public schools. My father attended public school, and my mother had gone to BIA. I was able to make my own choice as long as I took learning seriously. In my family, education was strongly stressed. I have always been surrounded by relatives who provided strong examples of what a quality education could render. My mother is a nurse, my uncle is an educator, another uncle is a surgeon, and many members of my extended family had gone on to earn college degrees.

"As the oldest, I was strongly urged to continue my education, so I embarked on a program that would include all the college preparatory classes I would need to ensure my entrance into a college or university. Even at the high school level, I enjoyed science and knew that would be my field of concentration.

"During the summer of my junior year in high school, I attended the Minority Introduction to Engineering course at New Mexico State University. I was exposed to all the different types of engineering. Civil engineering easily became my choice because I always loved the outdoors. I knew I wouldn't be happy sitting at a desk or computer all the time.

"After high school, I enrolled at New Mexico State, since I had received a positive introduction to its engineering program. In addition, my uncle worked there, I had friends going to school there, and it was my home state. Happily, I was awarded a four-year Professional Guild Scholarship from the U.S. Health Service. Thus, I became a freshman there in the fall of 1979. The scholarship paid for all my undergraduate education, but in return upon my graduation I was obligated to work for the agency for four years.

"After receiving my bachelor of science degree in environmental engineering, I was assigned to Tuba City, Arizona, on a Navajo Indian reservation. As a field engineer, I was responsible for planning and organizing the construction of sanitation facilities and bringing in water lines for individual families. I found it to be very rewarding work, and it seems that the Navajos agreed. When I left, they presented me with an achievement medal for the work I did during those four years.

"Another of my focuses is my membership in the Commission Corps of the Public Health Service, one of the branches of the military. We have uniforms just like the navy. Upon finishing my bachelor of science degree, I had a choice of entering as a civil service employee or applying for the Commission Corps. I elected to apply for the Commission Corps because I was told that I would probably advance more quickly that way. Today, I hold the rank of lieutenant commander.

"In August of 1988, I transferred to the Pacific Northwest and worked with three different tribes, assuming the same duties as I had previously. I was the only field engineer in the office, and it was kind of scary at first, but I learned to be independent. In 1991, I was selected engineer of the year for the Portland area.

"After three years, the Indian Health Service chose me for 'long-term' training to get my master's degree in environmental engineering. The offer allowed me to go to school for one year and still receive my regular yearly salary. All educational expenses were absorbed by the agency. I felt that this was such a wonderful offer, I could not turn it down.

"I returned to New Mexico State for my advanced degree. The only hard part is that you must finish in one year, and the program is really a two-year program. It's pretty difficult to keep up, but if you are dedicated to it, you will succeed."

Expert Advice

"You need to persevere. I was determined to get my degree no matter what. And I had some hard times in college where I thought, 'Oh, I'm not going to pass this class.' I used to worry about this, but I always managed to do all right. I relied on friends or sought out help from teachers. It's not easy, but nothing that's worth accomplishing ever is. Every time you reach a goal you've set for yourself, it's time to set another.

"When I went back for my master's degree (where you must maintain a B average or better), I realized I could have worked a lot harder as an undergraduate. You should always do the best you can. Just meeting minimum standards is not good enough."

FOR MORE INFORMATION

A number of engineering-technology-related organizations provide information on engineering technician and technology careers. The Junior Engineering Technical Society (JETS), at 1420 King St., Suite 405, Alexandria, VA 22314-2715, serves as a central distribution point for information from most of these organizations. Enclose a self-addressed, business-size envelope with four first-class stamps to obtain a sampling of materials available.

Nonhigh school students and those wanting more detailed information should contact societies representing the individual branches of engineering. Each can provide information about careers in the particular branch.

For information about aeronautical and aerospace engineering, send $3 to:

American Institute of Aeronautics and Astronautics, Inc., AIAA Student Programs, The Aerospace Center, 370 L'Enfant Promenade S.W., Washington, D.C. 20024-2518

For information about chemical engineering, contact:

American Institute of Chemical Engineers, 345 East 47th St., New York, NY 10017-2395

American Chemical Society, Career Services, 1155 16th St. N.W., Washington, D.C. 20036

For information about civil engineering, contact:

American Society of Civil Engineers, 345 E. 47th St., New York, NY 10017

For information about electrical and electronics engineering, contact:

Institute of Electrical and Electronics Engineers, 1828 L St. N.W., Suite 1202, Washington, D.C. 20036

For information about industrial engineering, contact:

Institute of Industrial Engineers, Inc., 25 Technology Park/Atlanta, Norcross, GA 30092

For information about mechanical engineering, contact:

The American Society of Mechanical Engineers, 345 E. 47th St., New York, NY 10017

American Society of Heating, Refrigerating, and Air-Conditioning Engineers, Inc., 1791 Tullie Circle N.E., Atlanta, GA 30329

For information about metallurgical, ceramic, and materials engineering, contact:

The Minerals, Metals, & Materials Society, 420 Commonwealth Dr., Warrendale, PA 15086-7514

ASM International, Student Outreach Program, Materials Park, OH 44073-0002

For information about mining engineering, contact:

> The Society for Mining, Metallurgy, and Exploration, Inc., P.O. Box 625002, Littleton, CO 80162-5002

For information about nuclear engineering, contact:

> American Nuclear Society, 555 North Kensington Ave., LaGrange Park, IL 60525

For information about petroleum engineering, contact:

> Society of Petroleum Engineers, 222 Palisades Creek Dr., Richardson, TX 75080

CHAPTER 5

Careers in Computer Science and Mathematics

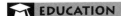 **EDUCATION**
B.A./B.S. required; postgraduate work recommended

$$$ SALARY
$20,000 to $70,000

OVERVIEW
Computer Scientists and Systems Analysts

The rapid spread of computers and computer-based technologies over the past two decades has generated a need for skilled, highly trained workers to design and develop hardware and software systems and to incorporate these advances into new or existing systems. Although many narrow specializations have developed and no uniform job titles exist, this professional specialty group is widely referred to as computer scientists and systems analysts.

Computer scientists generally design computers and conduct research to improve their design or use, as well as develop and adapt principles for applying computers to new uses. Computer scientists perform many of the same duties as other computer professionals throughout a normal workday, but their jobs are distinguished by the higher level of theoretical expertise and innovation they apply to complex problems and the creation or application of new technology. Computer scientists include computer engineers, database administrators, computer support analysts, and a variety of other specialized workers.

Computer scientists employed by academic institutions work in areas ranging from theory, to hardware, to language design. Some work on multidisciplinary projects; for example, developing and advancing uses for virtual reality. Their counterparts in private industry work in areas such as applying theory, developing specialized languages, or designing programming tools, knowledge-based systems, or computer games.

Computer engineers work with the hardware and software aspects of systems design and development. Computer engineers may often work as part of a team that designs new computing devices or computer-related equipment. Software engineers design and develop both packaged and systems software.

Database administrators work with database management systems software. They reorganize and restructure data to better suit the needs of users. They also may be responsible for maintaining the efficiency of the database and system security and may aid in design implementation.

Computer support analysts provide assistance and advice to users, interpreting problems and providing technical support for hardware, software, and systems. They may work within an organization or directly for the computer or software vendor.

Far more numerous, systems analysts use their knowledge and skills in a problem-solving capacity, implementing the means for computer technology to meet the individual needs of an organization. They study business, scientific, or engineering data processing problems and design new solutions using computers. This process may include planning and developing new computer systems or devising ways to apply existing systems to operations still completed manually or by some less efficient method. Systems analysts may design entirely new systems, including both hardware and software, or add a single new software application to harness more of the computer's power. Systems analysts work to help an organization realize the maximum benefit from its investment in equipment, personnel, and business processes.

Analysts begin an assignment by discussing the data processing problem with managers and users to determine its exact nature. Much time is devoted to clearly defining the goals of the system and understanding the individual steps used to achieve them so that the problem can be broken down into separate programmable procedures. Analysts then use techniques such as structured analysis, data modeling, information engineering, mathematical model building, sampling, and cost accounting to plan the system. Analysts must specify the files and records to be accessed by the system and design the processing steps, as well as the format for the output that will meet the users' needs. Once the design has been developed, systems analysts prepare charts and diagrams that describe it in terms that managers and other users can understand. They may prepare a cost-benefit and return-on-investment analysis to help management decide whether the proposed system will be satisfactory and financially feasible.

When a system is accepted, systems analysts may determine what computer hardware and software will be needed to set up the system or implement changes to it. They coordinate tests and observe initial use of the system to ensure it performs as planned. They prepare specifications, work diagrams, and structure charts for computer programmers to follow and then work with them to "debug," or eliminate errors from, the system.

Some organizations do not employ programmers; instead, a single worker called a programmer-analyst is responsible for both systems analysis and programming. As this becomes more commonplace, analysts will increasingly work with computer aided software engineering (CASE) tools and object-oriented programming languages, as well as client/server applications development and multimedia and Internet technology.

One obstacle associated with expanding computer use is the inability of different computers to communicate with one another. Many systems analysts are involved with connecting all the computers in an individual office, department, or establishment. This "networking" has many variations and may be referred to as local-area networks, wide-area networks, or multiuser systems, for example. A primary goal of networking is to allow users of microcomputers, also known as personal computers or PCs, to retrieve data from a mainframe computer and use it at their terminal. This connection also allows data to be entered into the mainframe from the PC.

Because up-to-date information (accounting records, sales figures, or budget projections, for example) is so important in modern organizations, systems analysts may be instructed to make the computer systems in each department compatible so that facts and figures can be shared. Similarly, electronic mail requires open pathways to send messages, documents, and data from one computer "mailbox" to another across different equipment and program lines. Analysts must design the gates in the hardware and software to allow free exchange of data, custom applications, and the computer power to process it all. They study the seemingly incompatible pieces and create ways to link them so that users can access information from any part of the system.

Systems analysts design new solutions to business, scientific, and engineering data processing problems.

A growing number of computer scientists and systems analysts are employed on a temporary or contract basis, or as consultants. For example, a company installing a new computer system may need the services of several systems analysts just to get the system running. Because not all of them would be needed once the system is functioning, the company might contract directly with the systems analysts themselves or with a temporary help agency or consulting firm. Such jobs may last from several months up to two years or more.

Mathematicians

Mathematics is one of the oldest and most basic sciences. Mathematicians create new mathematical theories and techniques involving the latest technology and solve economic, scientific, engineering, and business problems using mathematical knowledge and computational tools.

Mathematical work falls into two broad classes: theoretical (pure) mathematics and applied mathematics. However, these classes are not sharply defined and often overlap.

Theoretical mathematicians advance mathematical science by developing new principles and new relationships between existing principles of mathematics. Although they seek to increase basic knowledge without necessarily considering its practical use, this pure and abstract knowledge has been instrumental in producing or furthering many scientific and engineering achievements.

Applied mathematicians use theories and techniques such as mathematical modeling and computational methods to formulate and solve practical problems in business, government, engineering, and the physical, life, and social sciences. For example, they may analyze the mathematical aspects of computer and communications networks, the effects of new drugs on disease, the aerodynamic characteristics of aircraft, or the distribution costs or manufacturing processes of businesses. Applied mathematicians working in industrial research and development may develop or enhance mathematical methods when confronted with difficult problems. Some mathematicians, called cryptanalysts, analyze and decipher encryption systems designed to transmit national security-related information.

Mathematicians use computers extensively to analyze relationships among variables, solve complex problems, develop models, and process large amounts of data.

Much work in applied mathematics, however, is carried on by persons other than mathematicians. In fact, because mathematics is the foundation upon which many other academic disciplines are built, the number of workers using mathematical techniques is many times greater than the number actually designated as mathematicians. Engineers, computer scientists, physicists, and economists are among those who use mathematics extensively but have job titles other than mathematician. Some workers such as statisticians, actuaries, and operations research analysts actually are specialists in a particular branch of mathematics.

TRAINING
Computer Scientists and Systems Analysts

There is no universally accepted way to prepare for a job as a computer professional because employers' preferences vary depending on the work they need done. Prior work experience is very important. Many people develop advanced computer skills in other occupations in which they work extensively with computers and then transfer into computer occupations. For example, an accountant may become a systems analyst specializing in accounting systems development, or an individual may move into a systems analyst job after working as a computer programmer.

Employers almost always seek college graduates for computer professional positions; for some of the more complex jobs, persons with graduate degrees are preferred. Generally, a Ph.D., or at least a master's degree in computer science or engineering, is required for computer scientist jobs in research laboratories or academic institutions. Some computer scientists are able to gain sufficient experience for this type of position with only a bachelor's degree, but this is difficult. Computer engineers generally need a bachelor's degree in computer engineering, electrical engineering, or math. Computer support analysts may also need a bachelor's degree in a computer-related field, as well as significant experience working with computers, including programming skills.

For systems analyst or even database administrator positions, many employers seek applicants who have a bachelor's degree in computer science, information science, computer information systems, or data processing. Employers generally look for people who are familiar with programming languages and have broad knowledge of and experience with computer systems and technologies, regardless of their college major. Courses in computer programming or systems design offer good preparation for a job in this field. For jobs in a business environment, employers usually want systems analysts to have a background in business management or a closely related field, while a background in the physical sciences, applied mathematics, or engineering is preferred for work in scientifically oriented organizations.

Systems analysts must be able to think logically, have good communication skills, and like working with ideas and people. They often deal with a number of tasks simultaneously. The ability to concentrate and pay close attention to detail is important. Although both computer scientists and systems analysts often work independently, they also may work in teams on large projects. They must be able to communicate effectively with computer personnel such as programmers and managers, as well as with other staff who have no technical computer background.

Technological advances come so rapidly in the computer field that continuous study is necessary to keep skills up to date. Continuing education is usually offered by employers, hardware and software vendors, colleges and universities, or private training institutions. Additional training may come from professional development seminars offered by professional computing societies.

The Institute for Certification of Computing Professionals offers the designation of certified computing professional (CCP) to those who have at least four years of work experience as a computer professional, or at least two years of experience and a college degree. Candidates must pass a core examination testing general knowledge, plus exams in two specialty areas or in one specialty area and two computer programming languages. The Quality Assurance Institute awards the designation of certified quality analyst (CQA) to individuals who meet education and experience requirements, pass an exam, and endorse a code of ethics. Neither designation is mandatory, but professional certification may provide a job seeker a competitive advantage.

Systems analysts may be promoted to senior or lead systems analysts after several years of experience. Those who show leadership ability also can advance to management positions such as manager of information systems or chief information officer.

Computer engineers and scientists employed in industry may eventually advance into managerial or project leadership positions. Those employed in academic institutions can become heads of research departments or published authorities in their field. Computer professionals with several years of experience and considerable expertise in a particular area may choose to start their own computer consulting firms.

Mathematicians

A bachelor's degree in mathematics is the minimum education needed for prospective mathematicians. In the federal government, entry-level job candidates usually need to have a four-year degree with a major in mathematics or a four-year degree with the equivalent of a mathematics major (twenty-four semester hours of mathematics courses).

In private industry, job candidates generally need a master's or a Ph.D. degree to obtain jobs as mathematicians.

Most of the positions designated for mathematicians are in research and development labs as part of technical teams. These research scientists engage in either pure mathematical, or basic, research or in applied research focusing on developing or improving specific products or processes. The majority of bachelor's and master's degree holders in private industry work not as mathematicians but in related fields such as computer science, where they are called computer programmers, systems analysts, or systems engineers.

A bachelor's degree in mathematics is offered by most colleges and universities. Mathematics courses usually required for this degree are calculus, differential equations, and linear and abstract algebra. Additional coursework might include probability theory and statistics, mathematical analysis, numerical analysis, topology, modern algebra, discrete mathematics, and mathematical logic. Many colleges and universities urge or even require students majoring in mathematics to take several courses in a field that uses or is closely related to mathematics such as computer science, engineering, operations research, physical science, statistics, or economics. A double major in mathematics and another discipline such as computer science, economics, or one of the sciences is particularly desirable. A prospective college mathematics major should take as many mathematics courses as possible while in high school.

In 1994, about 240 colleges and universities offered a master's degree as the highest degree in either pure or applied mathematics; 195 offered a Ph.D. in pure or applied mathematics. In graduate school, students conduct research and take advanced courses, usually specializing in a subfield of mathematics. Some areas of concentration are algebra, number theory, real or complex analysis, geometry, topology, logic, and applied mathematics.

If you are employed in the area of applied mathematics, training in the field in which your mathematics background will be used is very important. Fields in which applied mathematics is used extensively include physics, actuarial science, engineering, and operations research. Of increasing importance are computer and information science, business and industrial management, economics, statistics, chemistry, geology, life sciences, and the behavioral sciences.

Mathematicians should have substantial knowledge of computer programming because most complex mathematical computation and much mathematical modeling is done by computer.

Mathematicians need good reasoning ability and persistence in order to identify, analyze, and apply basic principles to technical problems. Communication skills are also important, as mathematicians must be able to interact with others, including nonmathematicians, and discuss proposed solutions to problems.

JOB OUTLOOK
Computer Scientists and Systems Analysts

Computer scientists and systems analysts will be among the fastest growing occupations through the year 2005. In addition, tens of thousands of job openings will result annually from the need to replace workers who move into managerial positions or other occupations or who leave the labor force.

The demand for computer scientists and engineers is expected to rise as organizations attempt to maximize the efficiency of their computer systems. There will continue to be a need for increasingly sophisticated technological innovation. Competition will place organizations under growing pressure to use technological advances in areas such as office and factory automation, telecommunications technology, and scientific research. As the complexity of these applications grows, more computer scientists and systems analysts will be needed to design, develop, and implement the new technology.

As more computing power is made available to the individual user, more computer scientists and systems analysts will be required to provide support. As users develop more sophisticated knowledge of computers, they become more aware of the machine's potential and better able to suggest how computers could be used to increase their own productivity and that of the organization. Increasingly, users are able to design and implement more of their own applications and programs. As technology continues to advance, computer scientists and systems analysts will continue to need to upgrade their levels of skill and technical expertise, and their ability to interact with users will increase in importance.

The demand for networking to facilitate the sharing of information will be a major factor in the rising demand for systems analysts. Falling prices of computer hardware and software should continue to induce more small businesses to computerize their operations, further stimulating demand for these workers. In order to maintain a competitive edge and operate more cost effectively, firms will continue to seek out computer professionals who are knowledgeable about the latest technologies and able to apply them to meet the needs of businesses. A greater emphasis on problem solving, analysis, and client/server environments will also contribute to the growing demand for systems analysts.

Individuals with an advanced degree in computer science should enjoy very favorable employment prospects because employers are demanding a higher level of technical expertise. College graduates with a bachelor's degree in computer science, computer engineering, information science, or information systems should also experience good prospects for employment. College graduates without computer science majors who have had courses in computer programming, systems analysis, and other data processing areas, as well as training or experience in an applied field, should be able to find jobs as computer professionals. Those who are familiar with CASE tools, object-oriented and client/server programming, and multimedia technology will have an even greater advantage, as will individuals with significant networking, database, and systems experience. Employers should increasingly seek computer professionals who can combine strong programming and traditional systems analysis skills with good interpersonal and business skills.

Mathematicians

Employment of mathematicians is expected to increase more slowly than the average for all occupations through the year 2005. The number of jobs available for workers whose educational background is solely mathematics is not expected to increase significantly. Many firms engaged in civilian research and development that use mathematicians are not planning to expand their research departments much and, in some cases, may reduce them. Expected reductions in defense-related research and development will also affect mathematicians' employment, especially in the federal government. Those whose educational background includes the study of a related discipline will have better job opportunities. However, as advancements in technology lead to expanding applications of mathematics, more workers with a knowledge of mathematics will be required. Many of these workers have job titles that reflect the end product of their work rather than the discipline of mathematics used in that work.

Bachelor's degree holders in mathematics are usually not qualified for most jobs as mathematicians. However, those with a strong background in computer science, electrical or mechanical engineering, or operations research should have good opportunities in industry. Bachelor's degree holders who meet state certification requirements may become high school mathematics teachers.

Holders of a master's degree in mathematics will face very strong competition for jobs in theoretical research. However, job opportunities in applied mathematics and related areas such as computer programming, operations research, and engineering design in industry and government will be more numerous.

SALARIES
Computer Scientists and Systems Analysts

Median annual earnings of computer systems analysts and scientists who worked full time in 1994 were about $44,000. The middle 50 percent earned between $34,100 and $55,000. The lowest 10 percent earned less than $25,100, and the highest tenth earned more than $69,400. Computer scientists with advanced degrees generally earn more than systems analysts.

According to Robert Half International Inc., starting salaries in 1994 for systems analysts employed by large establishments employing more than fifty staff members ranged from $43,500 to $54,000. Salaries for those employed in small establishments ranged from $35,000 to $45,000. Starting salaries ranged from $51,000 to $62,000 for database administrators, and from $45,000 to $62,000 for software engineers.

In the federal government, the entrance salary for systems analysts who are recent college graduates with a bachelor's degree was about $18,700 a year in 1995; for those with a superior academic record, $23,200.

Mathematicians

According to a 1995 survey by the National Association of Colleges and Employers, starting salary offers for mathematics graduates with a bachelor's degree averaged about $30,000 per year, while those with a master's degree averaged $35,600. Starting salaries for mathematicians were generally higher in industry and government than in educational institutions. For example, the American Mathematical Society reported that, based on a 1994 survey, median annual earnings for new recipients of doctorates in research were $35,000; for those in government, median earnings were $45,500; and, for those in business and industry, median earnings were $52,500.

In the federal government in 1995, the average annual salary for mathematicians in supervisory, nonsupervisory, and managerial positions was $58,150; for mathematical statisticians, the average was $60,510; and for cryptanalysts, the average was $52,840.

Benefits for mathematicians tend to be similar to those offered to most professionals who work in office settings: vacation and sick leave, health and life insurance, and a retirement plan, among others.

RELATED FIELDS
Computer Scientists and Systems Analysts

Other workers who use research, logic, and creativity to solve business problems are computer programmers, financial analysts, urban planners, engineers, operations research analysts, management analysts, and actuaries.

Mathematicians

Other occupations that require a degree in or extensive knowl-edge of mathematics include actuary, statistician, computer programmer, systems analyst, systems engineer, and opera-tions research analyst. In addition, a strong background in mathematics facilitates employment in fields such as engi-neering, economics, finance, and physics.

INTERVIEW
Krista Jacobsen, Ph.D.
Senior Systems Engineer

Krista Jacobsen is Senior Systems Engineer at Amati Communications Corporation in San Jose, California. She received her bachelor of sci-ence degree in electrical engineering from the University of Denver and both her master of science in electrical engineering and Ph.D. from Stanford University.

What the Job Is Really Like

"My job is somewhat unusual and, hence, difficult to describe. The company considers me quite versatile for a Ph.D., and they know that I enjoy doing many difficult things, including tasks not traditionally associated with electrical engineers such as writing and public speaking and working on heavy technical problems. My particular responsibilities include designing and managing the company's web site; writing and running computer simulations to project the performance of our systems; investigating alternative solutions and design of new products; attending standards meetings (for which I write and present technical contributions); and offering technical support as necessary to the sales and marketing departments, which frequently requires travel to other companies or to con-ferences. On the road once or twice a month, I give presenta-tions and/or attend meetings. At the office, I spend a lot of time writing, as ideas are useless unless they can be commu-nicated to others. I often write internal documents explaining the problems I've been looking at, and the solutions that I and my colleagues prepare."

How Krista Jacobsen Got Started

"I was attracted to electrical engineering because I found those courses to be the most challenging I had ever encountered. I worked harder than I ever had in school, and the extra effort really paid off: not only did I graduate with all As in major courses, but I was awarded scholarships to an outstanding graduate school and also awarded graduate fellowships.

"While working on my Ph.D., I was employed at Amati as a consultant. When the time came to start interviewing for a postgraduation job, Amati was quick to make me an offer. I still interviewed at other companies but knew in advance that I wanted to stay here because the company had been very good to me. I felt a loyalty to stay and become part of their team."

Expert Advice

"My advice is to work hard so you can reap the rewards. Many people drop out of engineering programs because some of the courses seem so difficult. The key is to survive the nasty courses and excel in the courses you enjoy. The road gets easier and more interesting as you progress, and eventually you'll find out that a career in engineering is fun, rewarding, and challenging."

●   ●   ●

INTERVIEW
Carol Prochnow, M.S.
Senior Section Manager

Carol Prochnow is Senior Section Manager at Schlumberger Well Services. She received her bachelor of science degree in electrical and computer engineering from the University of Michigan in Ann Arbor and her master of science degree in computer science from Cornell in Ithaca, New York.

What the Job Is Really Like

"I am an engineering manager for about twenty people. We are responsible for the data acquisition and analysis software for a service industry called oil well logging, Schlumberger's core business. When an oil company drills a well, it isn't like in movies when a huge gusher begins to spew oil into the sky. In fact, they sometimes do not know if there are hydrocarbons, or where they are. Schlumberger is hired to perform a service where advanced sensors are lowered into the oil-well bore, connected via a 'wifeline' conducting cable to a computer system on the surface. My section is responsible for the 'middleware' software that sits on top of this computer's operating system. This software provides data acquisition, data management, task control, and graphics facilities to support different sensors. This software is loaded into the computer system either in a truck or an offshore unit.

"A typical day is split between dealing with E-mail, having meetings, reviewing documents, and talking on the phone. Sometimes, I really miss being an engineer so I'll go in and fix some software bug. However, I consider myself pretty dangerous in getting back into the code, since I do it so infrequently. But I love to build things, so I'm really glad that this is an integral part of my job.

"A day in the life of an engineer here is E-mail, web surfing, programming/debugging, writing/reviewing documents, and attending technical meetings. We take our projects all the way from requirements analysis through delivery to our field organization."

How Carol Prochnow Got Started

"When I was going to middle and high school, the computing profession was still in its infancy. My older brother was taking a class on the FORTRAN programming language, and I happened to look at the book and became fascinated by the whole idea of programming. I'd always loved math but didn't see a career there. Computer science, however, seemed very attractive and looked like a career that would be viable for many years."

Expert Advice

"I would advise interested candidates to get good grades. Grades are what you need to get your foot in the door of a good job. Schlumberger engineering does not even look at resumes that have less than a B+ average.

"Continuing your education is always a plus. And internships are very valuable. In my own case, I feel that my master's degree helped me to get this job and also provided me with some skills I didn't have when I finished my undergraduate program.

"It's a good idea to work at a variety of companies during summer breaks. You'll learn a lot and also find out if you like working with the same individuals day after day. If your experience is negative, engineering is probably not for you."

● ● ●

INTERVIEW
Steven Brent Assa, Ph.D.
Research Scientist

Steven Assa is a research scientist. He earned his bachelor of arts degree in mathematics and Scandinavian literature and his Ph.D. in mathematics from Ohio State University.

What the Job Is Really Like

"My current job is the most wonderful job that I can imagine. I may sound over the top on this, but over the past five years I have begun to see the beauty of mathematics in the physics applications that I work on at a level that makes me honored to think that I understand even a small part of their beauty and organic purpose.

"I spend about eight hours at my office, but I spend many more hours a day thinking about the meaning and elegance of the equations that I manipulate. My job is to build a three-dimensional geometry modeling system for geological applications. I work with geologists, physicists, computer scientists, and other mathematicians. There are never enough hours in the day for me to talk to all the people that I interact with.

"My typical day begins with answering mail and checking in with a junior colleague with whom I am working very closely. If he or I have questions regarding the previous day's collaboration, we review them. Otherwise, we decide what aspect of the project to consider, decide who looks at which issues, and then separate for a few hours. I make notes, decide how to approach my projects, and then close my door and get immersed. Interruptions break my concentration, but part of the fun of this job is the new issues being raised by users of the computer system that I have built.

"The work is very pleasant, but I do get mentally tired from this work. When this happens, I pull down one of the classical mathematical physics books that I have, to gain a sense of clarity and give myself a chance to avoid my immediate problems for a few minutes.

"In a sentence, I have a job that permits me to be a permanent graduate student research assistant, with myself as the boss.

"Most of all, I like the idea that I am able to propose the majority of my work. However, my work is not open-ended—far from it. I work on projects that have a very visible payoff for my company, but I am able to focus on the parts that are exciting to me. I am trusted and have the respect of my management. I have no managerial urge, and the company has not tried to force me into this level.

"The least agreeable part of what I do is to make certain that I am not drafted back into the day-to-day engineering ranks of the company. I did this for about nine years, and it was certainly good training in general computer systems design, product completion, and group effort, but today I need time to dream. Fortunately, after my first patent was issued, the company realized that my talents could be used more efficiently in my present position."

How Steven Brent Assa Got Started

"I have known since I was a child that I would be a scientist. When I was very small, I thought that meant that I would be a medical doctor (psychiatrist, to be exact). I held that belief until I got to college and discovered that what I really liked was mathematics and Scandinavian literature (Ibsen and Strindberg).

Mathematics appealed to me because I thought that God spoke to people through universal laws that were conveyed in goodness and love, through mathematical equations. Understanding these equations was the same as understanding the way the world is, which is a first step to accepting the beings in the world.

"I earned my B.A. in mathematics and Scandinavian literature in 1970 and my Ph.D. in mathematics in 1974 from Ohio State University in Columbus, Ohio."

Expert Advice

"I would recommend that you never lose your need to understand why things are the way they are. Talk to people about your ideas and spend your time trying to make something useful out of them. Read, read, read—especially the 'classics.' Clarity of thought is timeless and independent of the problem addressed."

● ● ●

INTERVIEW
Brian Killen, B.S.
Software Engineer

Brian Killen is a software engineer. He earned his bachelor of science degree in computer science from Kansas State University.

What the Job Is Really Like

"Our days are influenced by the projects we are working on at the time. The projects run on one- to two-year cycles. In the beginning of a project, there is a lot of thinking, designing, and talking to customers. The latter half of a project is spent sitting at the keyboard and writing code all day. (I would say 50 percent of the project is spent writing code.) It is the last five months of a project that are the busiest and most stressful.

"Our work atmosphere is extremely casual. I work in an office where the set hours are Monday through Friday from 8:30 A.M. until 5:00 P.M. However, the truth is that I usually work fifty to sixty hours per week. During crunch time, it can be seventy hours per week. It's a very intense job—definitely not low key.

"The staff convenes weekly meetings via teleconference, as some working on the projects are in California and India.

"What I like best is creating the products for people to use. What I like least is the turnaround time for a product. It takes two years to see end results, to feel the full gratification of the job."

How Brian Killen Got Started

"I became interested in computers while in high school. And, during college, I served in an internship with a computer services organization. I earned a bachelor of science degree in computer science from Kansas State University in Manhattan, Kansas. Further, I have enhanced my expertise by attending numerous seminars—anything to do with software engineering development. I have always wanted to develop products that help people communicate with each other."

Expert Advice

"In order to serve in this position effectively, you need experience in design user interfaces, software engineering skills, programming skills, networking, protocol development, C++ language, patience, the capacity to work in a team setting, the ability to keep the customer in mind, the skills required to work well with a diverse group of people, good communication and interpersonal habits, attention to detail, stamina to work on a project for years, persistence, and insight into where the industry is going.

"You really have to like this kind of work to do this job because it's quite demanding. Long, difficult, stressful hours are fairly common. I'd advise others to get as much experience as early as possible because this isn't a job you really come to understand in college. It's a job you learn by doing. Once you experience the doing, you'll be able to determine if this is something that you truly want to make your life's work."

● ● ●

INTERVIEW
Celeste M. Combs, M.S.
Human Factors Engineer

Celeste M. Combs is a human factors engineer for Microsoft. She earned her bachelor of arts degree in health education/kinesiology from the University of North Iowa, Cedar Falls, Iowa. She also studied biomechanics in the master of science program at the University of Oregon, Eugene, Oregon, and bioengineering in the master of science program at the University of Washington, Seattle, Washington.

What the Job Is Really Like

"On a daily basis, I conduct biomechanical and design-related research to improve hardware products such as the mouse, keyboard, and gaming products in order to optimize them on both a physical and mechanical basis. I interact with industrial designers, ergonomists, software engineers, mechanical and electrical engineers, and program managers. This position requires good communication and writing skills. Each product brings different challenges; however, my experience brings cumulative expertise to each situation.

"Like many jobs, there are deadlines, decisions, and generally very busy days. Within that context, I enjoy my job tremendously. I believe to work in these environments, people must enjoy what they do and be able to see a broader picture. When I see a product in someone's hand and also hear positive feedback, it brings me a tremendous reward."

How Celeste M. Combs Got Started

"I was attracted to the profession because I was focused on improving the lives of others. I had also been fascinated by human movement and performance most of my life. Biomechanics is science that applies physiology and mechanics to understanding movement. This helps improve performance and limits injury. However, I personally look at human beings as interacting within larger systems that not only encompass the physical realm but also cognitive and emotional areas. I envisioned working in a rewarding environment with a mission to optimize all these elements. In my current position at Microsoft, I feel fortunate to work within interdisciplinary teams to reach this larger goal of optimizing the systems within which we live and spend our time daily.

"Every work experience, including interacting with colleagues, has influenced my career path. The first year or so out of college, I worked in a business environment which was where I thought I wanted to be. However, I was really reacting to outside pressures rather than following my heart. However, the time proved valuable because I gained some applicable business skills that would later translate to any profession.

"I changed paths and decided to pursue physiology, gaining a valuable foundation needed for my current environment and graduate work. For five years before attending graduate school, I worked for three employers. These included a stint as a physical therapy assistant, another as a research assistant at the internationally renowned Institute for Aerobics Research in Dallas, and, finally, as research assistant in the research division of a pharmaceutical firm conducting and managing research projects around the country. All environments were beneficial and gave me experience and interaction with outstanding scientists and researchers. The cumulative experience of these positions provided me with the edge and insight required to do outstanding research and design work at Microsoft with an emphasis in human factors engineering."

Expert Advice

"I would advise that you get some experience so that you are sure that this is the profession for you. That's your first challenge. Once this has been established, I would stress that you have an open mind to alternatives.

"Remember that out of every rejection or negative situation, there are a host of alternatives and positive situations. So, it helps to be flexible. Education and knowledge are always a part of a process. You must realize that success won't come at once but slowly with experience and time. But you should always seek the courage to live your passion—whatever inspires and motivates you most."

• • •

INTERVIEW
Tom Teska, B.S.
Computer Consultant

Tom Teska is a computer consultant. He has worked in that capacity since 1980 and as a certified network engineer since 1991.

What the Job Is Really Like

"As a consultant and support person, the thing I like most is being able to get people's PCs to do things that no one else can do. People call me when they've got a problem that they haven't been able to solve, and I fix it for them. It makes me feel good to help them like that, and I enjoy the thanks I get from the users in those situations. I also look forward to the actual work with the computers. I have fun while I'm working.

"Presently, I am employed by a long-term contract consulting firm, and the pace is steady but not overwhelming. I report to only one client supporting less than 10,000 people and now work a standard forty-hour week. When I was assigned to commercial stores, there was no such thing as a typical day. That was actually one of the things I liked about it. I supported people in many different industries, as well as our internal staff. One day, I'd be working with bankers, and the next day I'd be helping teachers in an elementary school. Now that I support only one company, I do have typical days. I work in a cubicle with several other support people. We install and support applications and maintain the large WAN that is installed here. I also work on the second-level help desk, which means that I get the problem calls that the first-level people can't solve.

"When I worked in the commercial part of this field, I also got to work with cutting-edge technology. It was really enjoyable to work on new systems that no one had tried before. I find it particularly pleasurable to learn new things.

"My least favorite aspect of this business is having to solve the same problems over and over. Another minor annoyance is that every once in a while I run into a customer who isn't satisfied, no matter what I do for him or her. Luckily, this doesn't happen very often. Most of the time, people are very appreciative of my knowledge and my efforts."

How Tom Teska Got Started

"I earned a bachelor of science degree in computer science from the University of Wisconsin in Madison, Wisconsin, and have served as a consultant since 1980 and a certified network engineer since 1991. I also received training on Netware 4.x Administration and design and took a class on teaching Novell courses.

"My father opened a ComputerLand store in 1980. When we brought the computers in for his original stock, I started using them and discovered that I loved working on them and making them do things that no one else could do. From there, I went to helping people use them better. The consulting work lets me do this and work on computers—the best of both worlds.

"Over the years, my job has changed many times. When I worked in the commercial sector, I operated at a very high pace. My work with ComputerLand and Entre stores had me supporting upwards of 1,000 companies with tens of thousands of people. I was typically working sixty to eighty hours a week for months on end."

Expert Advice

"I feel that the most important thing about being a consultant is to keep learning. I think it's my job to know more about PCs, networks, and software than my customers. Thus, I constantly seek out new information through reading and enrolling in classes in order to be aware of the new strategies and technologies that come to light virtually every day in this ever-changing field."

●   ●   ●

INTERVIEW
Tim Lee, M.B.A.
Network Consultant

Tim Lee is a network consultant/LAN administrator for Anderson Consulting in Lincoln, Nebraska.

What the Job Is Really Like

"About half of my day is spent in day-to-day operations management, implementing changes to the system and finding solutions to ongoing problems. I spend about 30 percent of the day on the phone with clients, helping them solve their computer problems. The other 20 percent is spent documenting what I've done that day to help clients.

"In order to serve in this position, you need to have good problem-solving skills, PC and network experience, experience in customer service/relationship building, organizational skills, networking skills, and the ability to work in a team setting.

"Our company maintains an open-door policy. We perform our work at the client's site, so it's not exactly a casual setting. Our most hectic times are when the computer goes down or when new programs are being implemented. I work an average of forty to fifty hours per week, including some evenings.

"What I like best about this job is having the freedom to do what is best for the client. Management really encourages us to be creative with our ideas. We work very much in a team setting, which is nice. My boss has a very good hands-off management style. He trusts me to do what is best for the client. There is a strong entrepreneurial spirit here. I dislike working under the constraints of a state budget, as funds are limited, but, on the positive side, it presents challenges in offering the customer the most for the money that is available."

How Tim Lee Got Started

"I earned a bachelor of science degree in economics from Kansas State University in Manhattan, Kansas, and an M.B.A. from Kansas State University in Kansas City, Missouri.

"While working in mutual-fund processing, I developed computer system knowledge which led to me taking this job. Before this, I hadn't worked in the field of computers, although they have always interested me."

Expert Advice

"I'd advise prospective candidates to learn as much as you can about computer software and systems. It's important to develop great problem-solving and customer relationship skills. You have to be a people person. Gain experience as you study. Always keep in mind that your experience will help you in the future."

• • •

INTERVIEW
Jennifer Cahow
Mechanical Computer Aided Drafter

Jennifer Cahow is employed as a mechanical computer aided drafter.

What the Job Is Really Like

"Basically, my job consists of drawing mechanical gadgets on the computer. Occasionally, I get into other issues that allow me to leave my desk, like helping to put together the gadgets I draw. My job description can be summed up in one sentence: long hours spent in front of a computer drawing things in AutoCAD.

"I'm very happy in this career. I really like the location, the people, and the fact that I can draw on a computer. Computer-aided animation is something that interests me, and I'm an artist when not at work. I really like gadgets and picturing how they will go together in my mind, and then making it happen on the screen. My hours are pretty flexible here. I need to put in eight hours, but I can start and leave whenever I want. The only downside is that not everything I draw is exciting."

How Jennifer Cahow Got Started

"I am a high school graduate. I was a hand drafter previously (which I learned on the job). The occupation of hand drafter became out of date, so I had to get training on the computer. I tend to learn quickly and have a great affinity for computers and mechanical devices. So, it seemed like a perfect career. I enjoy both the job and the financial rewards."

Expert Advice

"If you like to draw on a computer, go for it. You can eventually get into design work, and that can do a lot for your brain. It's really quite a challenge. Still, for the most part, this job is for someone who doesn't want to lead (unless you get into the design aspect of it)."

FOR MORE INFORMATION

Further information about computer careers is available from:

Association for Computing Machinery, 1515 Broadway, New York, NY 10036

Information about the designation of certified computing professional is available from:

Institute for the Certification of Computing Professionals, 2200 East Devon Ave., Suite 268, Des Plaines, IL 60018

Information about the designation of certified quality analyst is available from:

Quality Assurance Institute, 7575 Dr. Phillips Blvd., Suite 350, Orlando, FL 32819

About the Author

Jan Goldberg's love for the printed page began well before her second birthday. Regular visits to the book bindery where her grandfather worked produced a magic combination of sights and smells that she carries with her to this day.

Childhood was filled with composing poems and stories, reading books, and playing library. Elementary and high school included an assortment of contributions to school newspapers. While a full-time college student, Goldberg wrote extensively as part of her job responsibilities in the College of Business Administration at Roosevelt University in Chicago. After receiving a degree in elementary education, she was able to extend her love of reading and writing to her students.

Goldberg has written extensively in the occupations area for General Learning Corporation's *Career World Magazine*, as well as for the many career publications produced by CASS Recruitment Publications. She has also contributed to a number of projects for educational publishers, including Scott Foresman and Addison-Wesley.

As a feature writer, Goldberg's work has appeared in *Parenting Magazine, Today's Chicago Woman, Opportunity Magazine, Chicago Parent, Complete Woman, North Shore Magazine*, and Pioneer Press newspapers. In all, she has published more than 250 pieces as a full-time freelance writer.

In addition to *On the Job: Real People Working in Science*, the other books she has written for NTC/Contemporary Publishing include *On the Job: Real People Working in Communications, Great Jobs for Music Majors, Great Jobs for Computer Science Majors, Careers for Courageous People, Careers in Journalism, Opportunities in Research and Development Careers*, and *Opportunities in Horticulture Careers*.